MATHEMATICS DICTIONARY

ALGORITHMS and RULES in MATHEMATICS
for SECONDARY STUDENTS

KATHLEEN TOWLER

The McGraw·Hill Companies

Sydney New York San Francisco Auckland
Bangkok Bogotá Caracas Hong Kong
Kuala Lumpur Lisbon London Madrid
Mexico City Milan New Delhi San Juan
Seoul Singapore Taipei Toronto

Text © 2004 McGraw-Hill Australia Pty Ltd
Illustrations and design © 2004 McGraw-Hill Australia Pty Ltd
Additional owners of copyright are named in on-page credits.

Apart from any fair dealing for the purposes of study, research, criticism or review, as permitted under the *Copyright Act*, no part may be reproduced by any process without written permission. Enquiries should be made to the publisher, marked for the attention of the Permissions Editor, at the address below.

Every effort has been made to trace and acknowledge copyright material. Should any infringement have occurred accidentally the authors and publishers tender their apologies.

Copying for educational purposes
Under the copying provisions of the *Copyright Act*, copies of parts of this book may be made by an educational institution. An agreement exists between the Copyright Agency Limited (CAL) and the relevant educational authority (Department of Education, university, TAFE, etc.) to pay a licence fee for such copying. It is not necessary to keep records of copying except where the relevant educational authority has undertaken to do so by arrangement with the Copyright Agency Limited.

For further information on the CAL licence agreements with educational institutions, contact the Copyright Agency Limited, Level 19, 157 Liverpool Street, Sydney NSW 2000. Where no such agreement exists, the copyright owner is entitled to claim payment in respect of any copies made.

Enquiries concerning copyright in McGraw-Hill publications should be directed to the Permissions Editor at the address below.

National Library of Australia Cataloguing-in-Publication data:

Towler, Kathleen.
Mathematics dictionary: algorithms and rules in mathematics for secondary students.

Includes index.
ISBN 0 074 71385 X.

1. Mathematics — Dictionary. I. Title.

510.3

Published in Australia by
McGraw-Hill Australia Pty Ltd
Level 2, 82 Waterloo Road, North Ryde NSW 2113
Acquisitions Editor: Laura Whitton
Production Editor: Sybil Kesteven
Editor: Carolyn Pike
Proofreader: Tim Learner
Designer (cover and interior): Peter Evans
Illustrators: Alan Laver, Shelly Communications
Typeset in 9/11 pt Berkeley by Post Pre-Press
Printed on 80 gsm woodfree by Pantech Limited, Hong Kong.

Contents

Note: Keystrokes for scientific and graphing calculators in the text are for Casio. Keystrokes for Texas Instruments (TI) scientific and graphing calculators for the same examples are listed on p. 135.

Signs and symbols — vi
Multiplication table — vi

Chapter 1   **Number**   **1**

     Place value — 1
     The four operations — 1
     Factors — 1
     Tests for divisibility — 2
     Working with zero and one — 3
     Commutative and associative laws — 3
     Order of operations — 4
     Integers — 4
     Approximation — 6
     Estimation — 7

Chapter 2   **Time**   **8**

     Time conversions and units — 8
     Calculator use and time — 8
     24-hour clock — 9
     Time differences — 10
     Australian time — 10
     World time zones — 11

Chapter 3   **Fractions**   **13**

     Fractions and place value — 13
     Improper fractions and mixed numbers — 13
     Equivalent fractions — 14
     Operations with common fractions — 15

Chapter 4   **Decimal fractions**   **19**

     Operations involving decimals — 19
     Multiplying decimals — 20
     Dividing decimals — 21
     Conversion from fraction to decimal — 22
     Conversion from decimal to fraction — 22
     Recurring decimals — 23
     Multiplying and dividing by powers of 10 — 23
     Irrational numbers — 23
     The real number system — 24

Chapter 5 — Percentages — 25
The meaning of per cent — 25
Linking percentage, decimals and fractions — 25
Percentage and money — 27

Chapter 6 — Points, lines, angles and plane figures — 30
Points and lines — 30
Angles — 31
Plane figures — 33
Triangles — 34
Quadrilaterals — 35
Circles — 36
Symmetry — 37

Chapter 7 — Algebra — 40
Algebraic terminology — 40
Power notation — 41
Algebra and the four operations — 41
The distributive law — 43
Factorising — 45
Substitution — 47
Algebraic simplification of rational expressions — 48

Chapter 8 — Solving linear equations — 51
Inverse operations — 51
Inequations — 55
Solving linear inequations — 56

Chapter 9 — Indices and surds — 58
Indices — 58
Surds — 61
Standard form (scientific notation) — 63

Chapter 10 — Ratio, rate, scale and proportion — 64
Ratio — 64
Rate — 66
Scale — 67
Proportion — 68

Chapter 11 — Functions — 70
The cartesian plane — 70
Ordered pairs and plotting points — 71
Linear functions — 72
Algebraic format for linear functions — 74
Linking ordered pairs and linear graphs — 74
Domain and range — 75
Gradient (slope) — 76
Forms of linear equations — 78
Methods of sketching a straight line — 79
Lines parallel to the axes — 82
Special lines and their gradients — 83
Distance formula — 84
Midpoint formula — 84
Simultaneous equations — 84

Chapter 12	**Non-linear functions**	**87**
	Algebraic format for non-linear functions	87
	Solving quadratic equations	88
	Sketching parabolas	89
Chapter 13	**Interest**	**92**
	Simple interest	92
	Compound interest	94
Chapter 14	**Measurement**	**96**
	Length	96
	Area	99
	Surface area	103
	Mass	105
	Capacity	106
	Volume	106
	Volume and surface area of pyramids	108
Chapter 15	**Right-angled triangles**	**111**
	Theorem of Pythagoras	111
	Naming the sides in a right-angled triangle	111
	The tangent ratio in a right-angled triangle	112
	Sine (sin) and cosine (cos) ratios	114
Chapter 16	**Earth geometry**	**116**
	The coordinate system for maps	116
	Distances between places on the same longitude	117
	Distances between places on the same latitude	118
	Bearings and compass points	118
Chapter 17	**Data**	**119**
	Types of data	119
	Properties of graphs	119
	Statistical measures	124
Chapter 18	**Probability**	**129**
	The language of probability	129
	Experimental probability	129
	Probability of an event	130
	Compound probabilities	131
	Complementary events	132
	TI calculator conversions	135

SIGNS AND SYMBOLS

Sign/symbol	Meaning
≈	approximately equal to: e.g. 2.989 ≈ 3
≠	inequality—is not equal to: e.g. 4 + 2 ≠ 7
≅ or ≡	is congruent to
≈ or ///	is similar to
⇔	is equivalent to
>	is greater than: e.g. 7 > 6 or 7 > 4 + 2
≥	is greater than or equal to: e.g. 6 ≥ 2; 5 + 1 ≥ 2; 2 + 1 ≥ 3
<	is less than: e.g. 6 < 7 or 4 + 2 < 7
≤	is less than or equal to: e.g. 6 ≤ 7; 5 + 1 ≤ 7; 2 + 1 ≤ 3
$\sqrt{}$	the square root of: e.g. $\sqrt{9} = 3$
$\sqrt[3]{}$	the cube root of: e.g. $\sqrt[3]{27} = 3$
@	at: e.g. 2 apples @ 6c each cost 12c
%	per hundred (percentage sign): e.g. 50% means 50 out of every 100
∴	therefore
:	is to or out of (ratio sign) e.g. $1 : 4 = \frac{1}{4}$

MULTIPLICATION TABLE

×	0	1	2	3	4	5	6	7	8	9	10	11	12	13	14	15
0	0	0	0	0	0	0	0	0	0	0	0	0	0	0	0	0
1	0	1	2	3	4	5	6	7	8	9	10	11	12	13	14	15
2	0	2	4	6	8	10	12	14	16	18	20	22	24	26	28	30
3	0	3	6	9	12	15	18	21	24	27	30	33	36	39	42	45
4	0	4	8	12	16	20	24	28	32	36	40	44	48	52	56	60
5	0	5	10	15	20	25	30	35	40	45	50	55	60	65	70	75
6	0	6	12	18	24	30	36	42	48	54	60	66	72	78	84	90
7	0	7	14	21	28	35	42	49	56	63	70	77	84	91	98	105
8	0	8	16	24	32	40	48	56	64	72	80	88	96	104	112	120
9	0	9	18	27	36	45	54	63	72	81	90	99	108	117	126	135
10	0	10	20	30	40	50	60	70	80	90	100	110	120	130	140	150
11	0	11	22	33	44	55	66	77	88	99	110	121	132	143	154	165
12	0	12	24	36	48	60	72	84	96	108	120	132	144	156	168	180
13	0	13	26	39	52	65	78	91	104	117	130	143	156	169	182	195
14	0	14	28	42	56	70	84	98	112	126	140	154	168	182	196	210
15	0	15	30	45	60	75	90	105	120	135	150	165	180	195	210	225

1 Number

The **natural numbers** are the first set of numbers that we use. They are represented by digits such as 1, 2, 3, 4, 5, 6 . . . There is no end to these numbers and so they are said to be **infinite**.

Natural numbers are used for counting a number of objects. They are also used to order objects in statements such as 'She is the fourth student to complete her work', or to compare quantities in statements such as 'There are 5 more boys studying Art this year'.

When the number zero (0) is added to this set, these numbers are called the **whole numbers**. Hence, the whole numbers are 0, 1, 2, 3, 4, 5 . . .

PLACE VALUE

Our system of numbers is based on a **place value** concept. This means that a digit's meaning depends on the place that it is positioned in the number. The value of 3 in the number 302 is different to the value of 3 in the number 23.

Place value is organised as follows:

Wholes						
Millions	Hundred thousands	Ten thousands	Thousands	Hundreds	Tens	Units
1 000 000	100 000	10 000	1000	100	10	1

Example

The number 5 923 048 = 5 923 048 = 5 000 000 + 900 000 + 20 000 + 3 000 + 40 + 8

THE FOUR OPERATIONS

The four operations are **addition**, +, **subtraction**, −, **multiplication**, × and **division**, ÷.

Sums and differences

To find a **sum** is to add numbers. The sum of 6 + 1 is 7. To find a **difference** is to *subtract* numbers. The difference of 10 − 3 is 7. The numbers added or subtracted are called **terms**.

Addition is the *inverse* operation of subtraction. The opposite of adding a number is to subtract a number.

Products and quotients

To find a **product** is to multiply numbers. The product of 9 × 2 is 18. The numbers being multiplied are called **factors**.

To find a **quotient** is to divide numbers. The quotient of 12 ÷ 3 is 4. The **dividend** is the number being divided, or the *first* number. The number by which we divide, or the *second* number, is called the **divisor**. Hence, for the example 12 ÷ 3, the dividend is 12 and the divisor is 3.

Multiplication is the *inverse* operation of division. The opposite of multiplying by a number is to divide by a number.

FACTORS

Odd numbers are those numbers not divisible by 2. Odd numbers end in 1, 3, 5, 7 or 9. An algebraic expression for an odd number is $2n + 1$ where n is an integer.

Even numbers are divisible by 2. An algebraic expression for an even number is $2n$ where n is an integer.

Prime numbers have no factors except themselves and 1. **Example:** 2, 3, 5, 13, 29, 31.

Composite numbers have more than two factors. The number 4 is a composite number—its factors are 1 and 4, and 2 and 2.

One is neither a prime number nor a composite number.

A **factor** is a number that divides exactly into another number, without a remainder. The number 8 is a factor of 24 since $24 \div 8 = 3$; 7 is not a factor of 23 since $23 \div 7 = 3$ remainder 2.

Prime factors are all the prime numbers that multiply together to give the number. The prime factors of 18 are: 2, 3 and 3 since $2 \times 3 \times 3 = 18$.

The smallest common multiple is called the **lowest common multiple (LCM)**. **Example:** 40 is the LCM of 5 and 8 since it is the smallest number that has both 5 and 8 as its factors.

The **highest common factor (HCF)** of two or more numbers is the common factor that is the greatest. Considering the factors of 8 and 24:

The factors of 8 are 1, 2, 4, **8**
The factors of 24 are 1, 2, 3, 4, 6, **8**, 12, 24 } Hence, the HCF of 8 and 24 is 8.

A **multiple** of a number has that number as a factor. Consider the multiples of 2 and 5.

Multiples of 2: 2, 4, 6, 8, **10**, 12, ...
Multiples of 5: 5, **10**, 15, 20, ... } A common multiple of 2 and 5 is 10.

TESTS FOR DIVISIBILITY

- A number is *divisible by* 2 if it ends in 0, 2, 4, 6 or 8; that is, if it is even.
- A number is *divisible by* 3 if the sum of its digits is divisible by 3.

Example

621   Sum of the digits $= 6 + 2 + 1 = 9$
9 is divisible by 3 since $9 \div 3 = 3$
Hence, 621 is divisible by 3.

- A number is *divisible by* 4 if the number formed by its last two digits is divisible by 4.

Example

624   The number formed by the last two digits, 24, is divisible by 4 since $24 \div 4 = 6$.
Hence, 624 is divisible by 4.

- A number is *divisible by* 5 if its last digit is 5 or 0.

Example

55, 60

- A number is *divisible by* 6 if (a) it is even *and* (b) the sum of its digits is divisible by 3.

Example

570   $5 + 7 + 0 = 12$, which is divisible by 3 since $12 \div 3 = 4$
570 is even
Hence, 570 is divisible by 6.

- There is no easy divisibility test for 7.
- A number is *divisible by* 8 if the number formed by its last three digits is divisible by 8.

Example

328 248   248 is divisible by 8 since $248 \div 8 = 31$
Hence, 248 is divisible by 8.

- A number is *divisible by 9* if the sum of its digits is divisible by 9.

> **Example**
>
> 927   9 + 2 + 7 = 18
> 18 is divisible by 9 since 18 ÷ 9 = 2
> Hence, 927 is divisible by 9.

- A number is *divisible by 10* if the last digit is 0.

> **Example**
>
> 100, 10, 50

WORKING WITH ZERO AND ONE

- $\frac{0}{a} = 0;\ \frac{0}{26} = 0$ 0 divided by any number = 0.
- $\frac{0}{0}$ is *indeterminate*.   Any answer will suffice.
- $\frac{a}{0}$ is *undefined*; $\frac{76}{0}$ is undefined   Any number divided by 0 is undefined.
- $0 \times a = 0;\ 0 \times 10 = 0$ Any number times 0 = 0.
- $0 + a = a;\ 0 + 10 = 10$ If 0 is added to any number, it remains unchanged.
- $a - 0 = a;\ 10 - 0 = 10$ If 0 is subtracted from any number, it remains unchanged.
- $\frac{a}{1} = a;\ \frac{10}{1} = 10$ Any number divided by 1 remains unchanged.
- $a \times 1 = a;\ 10 \times 1 = 10$ Any number multiplied by 1 remains unchanged.

COMMUTATIVE AND ASSOCIATIVE LAWS

The table below shows which operations can be manipulated with turnarounds and grouping with brackets.

	Turnarounds (commutative law)	Grouping (associative law)
+	$a + b = b + a$ Example: $3 + 2 = 2 + 3$	$(a + b) + c = a + (b + c)$ Example: $(3 + 2) + 1 = 3 + (2 + 1)$
−	$a - b \neq b - a$ Example: $3 - 2 \neq 2 - 3$ Hence, subtraction is not commutative.	$(a - b) - c \neq a - (b - c)$ Example: $(3 - 2) - 1 \neq 3 - (2 - 1)$ Hence, subtraction is not associative.
×	$a \times b = b \times a$ Example: $3 \times 2 = 2 \times 3$	$(a \times b) \times c = a \times (b \times c)$ Example: $(3 \times 2) \times 6 = 3 \times (2 \times 6)$
÷	$a \div b \neq b \div a$ Example: $6 \div 2 \neq 2 \div 6$ Hence, division is not commutative.	$(a \div b) \div c \neq a \div (b \div c)$ Example: $(12 \div 6) \div 3 \neq 12 \div (6 \div 3)$ Hence, division is not associative.

ORDER OF OPERATIONS

When there is more than one operation in a calculation, they must be done in a set order:
1. Start from the left.
2. Work brackets from the inside out.
3. Multiplication and division next, whichever comes first.
4. Then addition and subtraction, whichever comes first.

Note: If you put these types of questions into your scientific calculator exactly as written, including the brackets, the calculator will complete the question in the correct order.

Example

Evaluate $5 + 6 \times 4 \div (8 - 6) - 1$.

Solution

$5 + 6 \times 4 \div (8 - 6) - 1$
$= 5 + 6 \times 4 \div 2 - 1$ *Bracket first.*
$= 5 + 24 \div 2 - 1$ *Multiplication comes before division.*
$= 5 + 12 - 1$ *Division is done before addition and subtraction.*
$= 17 - 1$ *Addition comes before subtraction in this question.*
$= 16$

Example

Evaluate $27 \div 3 \times [27 + (7 - 5)]$

Solution

$27 \div 3 \times [27 + (7 - 5)]$
$= 27 \div 3 \times [27 + 2]$ *Inside brackets first.*
$= 27 \div 3 \times 29$ *Outside brackets next.*
$= 9 \times 29$ *Division comes first in this question.*
$= 261$

INTEGERS

So far, we have looked at natural numbers and whole numbers. The set of numbers called the **integers** represent positive and negative whole numbers. A bank account debit of –$25 is an example of a use of an integer. Another is when the temperature is –12°C, which means 12° below zero.
The integers are the numbers . . . –5, –4, –3, –2, –1, 0, 1, 2, 3, 4, 5, 6 . . .
Like the natural and whole numbers, integers are *infinite*—there is no smallest or largest integer.
Every **positive integer** has a *corresponding* **negative integer**, as in 3 and –3, or –6 and 6.
When entering negative integers into a *computer*, they are usually entered with a *bracket*, as in (–8).
The number line below shows all the integers from –12 to 12.

To move in a **positive** direction, go to the **right**. To move in a **negative** direction, go to the **left**.

Adding and subtracting integers

Example

Evaluate 9 − 5.

Solution

Imagine that △ represents 1 and ▼ represents −1. Hence, △ + ▼ = 0.
9 − 5 is represented by △△△△△△△△△▼▼▼▼▼   This is 9 ones and 5 negative ones.
Every *pair* of △ + ▼ = 0. Therefore, 9 − 5 is shown by:
△△△△△△△△△
▼▼▼▼▼   which equals 4.
Hence, 9 − 5 = 4.

Integer Problem	Diagram	Answer	Notes and calculator steps (for Casio and Sharp)
−3 + 2	▼▼▼ △△	−1	Calculator steps: 3 ± + 2 =
6 − −2 = 6 + 2	△△△△△△ △△	8	− −a = a; 6 − −2 = 6 + 2 Two negatives following each other make a positive. Calculator steps: 6 − 2 ± =
5 − 4	△△△△△ ▼▼▼▼	1	Subtracting a number is the same as adding its opposite. a − b = a + −b; 5 − 4 = 5 + −4 Calculator steps: 5 − 4 =
2 − 5	△△ ▼▼▼▼▼	−3	Calculator steps: 2 − 5 =
−7 + −2	▼▼▼▼▼▼▼ ▼▼	−9	Calculator steps: 7 ± + 2 ± =

Multiplying and dividing integers

Multiplication

- If an *odd* number of negatives are multiplied, the answer is *negative*.

Example

−2 × 4 = −8   *one negative, answer negative*
−2 × −3 × −4 = −24   *three negatives, answer negative*

- If an *even* number of negatives are multiplied, the answer is *positive*.

Example

−2 × −4 = 8   *two negatives, answer positive*
−2 × −3 × −4 × −5 = 120   *four negatives, answer positive*

Division

- If an *odd* number of negatives are divided, the answer is *negative*.

Example

$-2 \div 4 = -\frac{1}{2}$ or $-\frac{2}{4} = -\frac{1}{2}$

$-24 \div -3 \div -2 = -4$

- If an *even* number of negatives are divided, the answer is *positive*.

Example

$-4 \div -2 = 2$

$-120 \div -10 \div -2 \div -3 = 2$

APPROXIMATION

Approximation is a *nearly* exact answer that is good enough in the context. The main technique for approximation is rounding. The *sign* for an answer being approximately equal to another is '≈'.

Rounding

Rounding means reducing the number of non-zero digits in a number to a particular place value. After a place value has been chosen, the next digit to the right is examined. If this digit is greater than or equal to 5, the digit in the chosen place is *rounded up by 1*. If the digit is less than 5, the digit in the chosen place *remains the same*.

Example

Round 27 472 to the nearest 100.

Solution

This means that we want zeros in all places after the hundreds place.

Write 27 ↓472 with an arrow above the place we are rounding to.   *Here, the 4 is in the hundreds place.*

The next number along from 4 is 7. This is greater than 5 so we add 1 to the 4. The answer is 27 500.

Example

Round 6.1238 to the nearest tenth.

Solution

We want zeros in every place after the tenths.

Write 6.↓1238 with the arrow above the tenths place.   *Here 1 is in the tenths place.*

The next number along from 1 is 2. This is less than 5 and so we don't add 1. The answer is 6.1000 = 6.1.

ESTIMATION

Estimation means making a *good guess* of a measure or number.

Example

How many women are at the meeting?

Solution
1. Group part of the picture as shown.
2. Count the number in the group. There are 18 women in the group.
3. Multiply by the number of groups.

There are four groups so the estimate is $4 \times 18 = 72$.

2 Time

TIME CONVERSIONS AND UNITS

Time conversions
60 seconds (s) = 1 minute
60 minutes (min) = 1 hour
24 hours (h) = 1 day
7 days (d) = 1 week
14 days = 1 fortnight
52 weeks and 1 day = 1 year
365 days = 1 year
366 days = 1 leap year
12 calendar months = 1 year
13 4-week months = 1 year
26 weeks = $\frac{1}{2}$ year
10 years (y) = 1 decade
100 years = 1 century
1000 years = 1 millennium
am = morning
pm = afternoon
noon = 12.00 pm
midnight = 12.00 am

Days In The Month
Thirty days have September,
April, June and November.
All the rest have thirty-one,
Except February alone,
Which has twenty-eight days clear,
And twenty-nine in each leap year.

Example

(a) How many minutes in 3 hours and 10 minutes?
(b) How many hours in $2\frac{1}{2}$ weeks?

Solution

(a) $3 \times 60 + 10$
  = 180 + 10
  = 190 min

(b) In $2\frac{1}{2}$ weeks there are (7 + 7 + 3.5) days = 17.5 d.

Each day has 24 hours. So, the number of hours in $2\frac{1}{2}$ weeks = 17.5×24 = 420 h.

Example

How many days between 15 November and Christmas Day?

Solution

November has 30 days and so there are 15 days until the end of November.
Christmas day is 25 December.
Number of days until Christmas = 15 + 25 = 40 d.

CALCULATOR USE AND TIME

Scientific calculators have a button that helps conversions between seconds, minutes and hours. It is usually marked as D°M'S (Sharp) or ° ′ ″ (Casio).

Example

Convert 210 minutes to hours and minutes.

Solution

There are 60 minutes in each hour, hence 210 ÷ 60 = 3.5 h.
To answer in hours and minutes express 0.5 h in minutes.
Half of 1 h = 30 min. So, the answer is 3 h 30 min.

This can be done far more easily using the calculator.
Calculator steps 210 ÷ 60 [2ndF] [D°M'S] = 3°30′, which is 3 h 30 min in a time context

Example

Convert 7589 seconds to hours, minutes and seconds.

Solution

There are 60 × 60 = 3600 seconds in 1 hour. Can any of the 7589 seconds can be named as hours?
There are two lots of 3600 in 7589: 2 × 3600 + 389 = 2 h 389 s.
There are 60 seconds in 1 minute. Can any of the 389 seconds can be named as minutes?
There are six lots of 60 in 389: 6 × 60 + 29 = 6 min 29 s.
So, the answer is 2 h 6 min 29 s.

Calculator steps: 7589 ÷ 3600 [2ndF] [D°M'S] = 2° 6′ 29, which is 2 h 6 min 29 s in a time context

Example

(a) Convert 3 min 15 s to *minutes* as a decimal.
(b) Convert 3 min 15 s to *hours* as a decimal.

Solution

(a) 15 seconds = $\frac{15}{60}$ = 0.25 min

So, the answer is 3.25 min.

Calculator steps: Press 3 [D°M'S] 15 [D°M'S] [2ndF] [D°M'S] = 3.25

Or press 3 [° ′ ″] 15 [° ′ ″] and the decimal equivalent appears on the screen

(b) First express 3 min 15 s in one unit.
3 min 15 s = (3 × 60 + 15) s
= 195 s.
There are 3600 seconds in 1 hour.
195 seconds = $\frac{195}{3600}$ = 0.05420 h
So, the answer is 0.0542 h.

Calculator steps: The main change is to enter the information with hours as well:

Press 0 [D°M'S] 3 [D°M'S] 15 [D°M'S] [2ndF] [D°M'S] = 0.0542 h

or press 0 [° ′ ″] 3 [° ′ ″] 15 [° ′ ″] and the decimal equivalent appears on the screen

24-HOUR CLOCK

Instead of using 'am' and 'pm', or 12-hour time, to give time, the hours in the day can be numbered from 1 to 24. Four digits are used to show the number of hours and the number of minutes. For example, 1.05 pm is 1305.

To convert from am and pm to 24-hour time *add 12* to any pm times.
To convert from 24-hour time to am and pm *subtract 12* from any times greater than 12.

Example

Convert to 24-hour time:
(a) 5.10 pm
(b) 2.30 am

Solution
(a) 5.10 pm = 5.10 + 12.00 = 1710
(b) 2.30 am = 0230

Example

Convert to normal time:
(a) 2315
(b) 0325

Solution
(a) 2315 = 23.15 − 12.00 = 11.15 pm
(b) 0325 = 3.25 am

TIME DIFFERENCES

When finding time differences, work in *whole hours* first.

Example

Find the hours worked by a night-shift employee who works from 7.25 pm to 4.55 am.

Solution

7.25 pm ⟶ 12.25 am ⟶ 4.25 am ⟶ 4.55 am
      5 hours   4 hours   30 minutes

Total time = 5 h + 4 h + 30 min = 9 h 30 min

Example

Find the hours worked from 8.25 am to 3.20 pm.

Solution

8.25 am ⟶ 2.25 pm ⟶ 3.20 pm   *We can't go to 3.25 pm since this*
  4 hours + 2 hours   35 minutes + 20 minutes   *is past the end of the work day.*

Total time = 6 h + 55 min = 6 h 55 min

Example

Find the hours elapsed from 0230 on Monday to 1650 on Tuesday.

Solution

0230 Monday ⟶ 0230 Tuesday ⟶ 1650 Tuesday
    1 day   14 hours + 20 minutes

Total time is 1 d 14 h 20 min.

AUSTRALIAN TIME

Because the Earth rotates, some parts of it face the Sun and are in daylight while other parts are in darkness at night. Hence, there are different times in different places. For example, the time in Brisbane is different to the time in Perth. For convenience, Australia has been divided into **time zones**.

Winter time

During winter, Australia is divided into three time zones:
- Eastern Standard Time (EST)
- Central Standard Time (CST) = EST $- \frac{1}{2}$ hour
- Western Central Time (WST) = EST $- 2$ hours

These time zones are shown in the figure opposite.

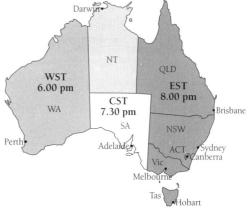

Australian time zones—Standard

Example

(a) If it is 10 am in Brisbane in winter, what time is it in Adelaide?

(b) If it is 1300 in Perth in winter, what is the time in Canberra in 12-hour time?

Solution

(a) Adelaide is on CST and so it is $10 - \frac{1}{2} = 9.30$ am in Adelaide.

(b) Perth is 2 hours behind Canberra and so Canberra time = 1300 + 0200 = 1500.
In 12-hour time this is 1500 − 1200 = 3 pm

Summer time

During summer, Australia is divided into five time zones:
- Eastern Standard Time (EST)
- Eastern Daylight Saving Time (EDT) = EST + 1 hour
- Central Standard Time (CST) = EST $- \frac{1}{2}$ hour
- Central Daylight Saving Time (CDT) = EST $+ \frac{1}{2}$ hour
- Western Standard Time (WST) = EST − 2 hours

These time zones are shown in the figure opposite.

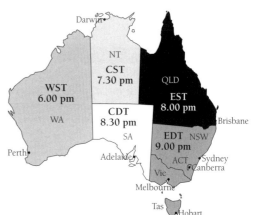

Australian time zones—Summer

Example

(a) If it is 1 pm in Brisbane in summer, what time is it in Sydney?

(b) If it is 2300 in Darwin in summer, what time is it in Hobart?

Solution

(a) Sydney is 1 hour ahead of Brisbane in summer, so it is 2 pm.

(b) Darwin is $1\frac{1}{2}$ hours behind Hobart during summer and so it is 2300 − 0130 = 2130 in Hobart.

WORLD TIME ZONES

World time zones are based on a comparison with the time at Greenwich (near London). The time at Greenwich is called GMT, or Greenwich Mean Time.

- Places that are *east* of Greenwich are *ahead* of its time.
- Places that are *west* of Greenwich are *behind* its time.

The time zones across the world are shown in the figure below.

Time displayed in black reflects standard time (ST) in the Northern and Southern Hemispheres

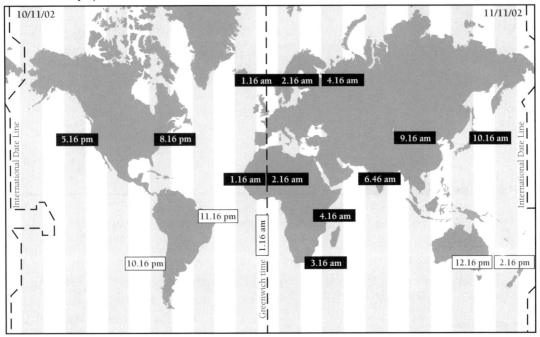

Example

(a) If it is 12 noon in Greenwich in November, what time is it in Brisbane?
(b) If it is 12 noon in Greenwich, what time is it in New York?
(c) Set up a table showing times in San Francisco, London and Brisbane to determine a time for a company to conduct a teleconference in November.
(d) It is 10 am on Sunday in Brisbane in November. What time is it in Tokyo?

Solution

(a) Brisbane = 12 noon + 10 hours = 10 pm
(b) New York = 12 noon − 5 hours = 7 am
(c)

San Francisco	London	Brisbane
4 am (Monday)	12 noon (Monday)	10 pm (Monday)
6 am	2 pm	12 midnight
8 am	4 pm	2 am
10 am	6 pm	4 am
12 noon	8 pm	6 am
2 pm	10 pm	8 am

The companies in these three cities could conduct a teleconference around 9 pm GMT.

(d) Tokyo is 1 hour behind Brisbane. So, if it is 10 am on Sunday in Brisbane, it is 9 am on Sunday in Tokyo.

3 Fractions

Questions such as 8 ÷ 2 have an answer which is a whole number: 8 ÷ 2 = 4. The question 2 ÷ 8 results in an answer which is less than one. Thus, $2 \div 8 = \frac{2}{8}$. The answer is a **fraction**—it is less than 1. This number, $\frac{2}{8}$, belongs to the set of **rational numbers**. Rational numbers are those numbers that can be expressed in the form of $\frac{p}{q}$ where p and q are integers and $q \neq 0$.

The rational number $\frac{3}{5}$ is also called a common fraction and can be modelled in many ways. Two of these ways are: ●●●○○

or

$$\begin{array}{cccccc} \frac{0}{5} & \frac{1}{5} & \frac{2}{5} & \frac{3}{5} & \frac{4}{5} & \frac{5}{5} \end{array}$$

The **denominator** is the number of divisions of the whole. The **numerator** tells the number of equal parts. In the fraction $\frac{3}{5}$, the denominator is 5 and the numerator is 3. The **vinculum** is the name given to the line that separates these. It means to bracket everything over and under the line and divide. Some examples of this include:

(a) $\frac{3}{5} = 3 \div 5$ (b) $\frac{8}{3-1} = 8 \div (3-1)$ (c) $\frac{8-3}{2} = (8-3) \div 2$

Thus, there are three ways of writing division: $5\overline{)3}$; $\frac{3}{5}$ (sometimes written as $3/5$) and $3 \div 5$.

FRACTIONS AND PLACE VALUE

Place value that includes fractions is organised as follows:

Wholes		Parts		
Tens	Units	Tenths	Hundredths	Thousandths
10	1	$\frac{1}{10}$	$\frac{1}{100}$	$\frac{1}{1000}$

Example

The number $18\frac{279}{1000} = 18 + \frac{2}{10} + \frac{7}{100} + \frac{9}{1000}$.

IMPROPER FRACTIONS AND MIXED NUMBERS

The fractions considered so far have been proper fractions. A **proper fraction** is less than 1. Its numerator is always smaller than the denominator, such as in $\frac{3}{4}$.

An **improper fraction** is equal to or greater than 1. Its numerator is the same as, or greater than, the denominator, such as in $\frac{9}{4}$ and $\frac{4}{4}$.

A fraction can also be expressed as a **mixed number**. It has a whole number part and a fraction part, such as in $2\frac{3}{4}$. i.e. $1 + 1 + \frac{3}{4}$

Converting from a mixed number to an improper fraction

Example

Convert $1\frac{3}{4}$ to an improper fraction.

Solution

$$1\frac{3}{4} = \frac{1 \times 4 + 3}{4}$$
$$= \frac{7}{4}$$

Converting from an improper fraction to a mixed number

Example

Convert the following to a mixed number:

(a) $\frac{7}{4}$ (b) $\frac{4}{4}$

Solution

(a) $\frac{7}{4}$
$= 7 \div 4$
$= 1 \text{ remainder } 3$
$= 1\frac{3}{4}$ Note that the 4 stays as the denominator.

Calculator steps: 7 $\boxed{a^{b}/_{c}}$ 4 $= 1 \rfloor 3 \rfloor 4 = 1\frac{3}{4}$

(b) $\frac{4}{4} = 1$

Calculator steps: 4 $\boxed{a^{b}/_{c}}$ 4 = 1

EQUIVALENT FRACTIONS

Equivalent fractions have the *same value* and represent the same proportion.

      $\frac{1}{2} = \frac{1}{2} \times \frac{2}{2} = \frac{2}{4}$ $\frac{2}{2} = 1$

For equivalent fractions, the *numerator* and *denominator* are *multiplied* or *divided* by the same number to make them equal. As the same number is multiplied, this is the same as multiplying by 1 and so there is no change in value.

The smallest equivalent fraction of a group is said to be in **lowest terms**. For the equivalent fractions $\frac{1}{2}, \frac{2}{4}, \frac{3}{6}$ and $\frac{4}{8}$, the lowest terms fraction is $\frac{1}{2}$.

Calculator steps: 4 $\boxed{a^{b}/_{c}}$ 8 $= 1 \rfloor 2 = \frac{1}{2}$.   *The same steps can be applied to any fraction in the list to reach this result.*

Equivalent fractions with like denominators

Equivalent fractions are used to find **like denominators**. For example, $\frac{2}{4}$ and $\frac{3}{4}$ have a like denominator of 4. Like denominators are needed if fractions are to be *compared*.

Example

Find x in the following, thus making equivalent fractions.

(a) $\dfrac{3}{12} = \dfrac{9}{x}$ (b) $\dfrac{5}{15} = \dfrac{x}{3}$

Solution

(a) $\dfrac{3}{12} = \dfrac{9}{x}$ *How do we get from 3 to 9 in the numerator? Multiply by 3. Do the same to the denominator.*

$\dfrac{3}{12} \times \dfrac{3}{3} = \dfrac{9}{36}$ $\dfrac{3}{3} = 1$.   *To multiply by 1 does not change the value of the fraction.*

$\therefore \quad x = 36$

(b) $\dfrac{5}{15} = \dfrac{x}{3}$ *How do we get from 15 to 3 in the denominator? Divide by 5. Do the same to the numerator.*

$\dfrac{5 \div 5}{15 \div 5} = \dfrac{1}{3}$ $\dfrac{5}{5} = 1$.   *To divide by 1 does not change the value of the fraction.*

$\therefore \quad x = 1$

OPERATIONS WITH COMMON FRACTIONS

Most fraction questions should be done using the *calculator*. Some ways of completing fraction questions with and without a calculator are given below.

Adding and subtracting fractions

Fractions must have like denominators to be added or subtracted.

Example

Evaluate $\dfrac{1}{4} + \dfrac{2}{4}$.

Solution

$\dfrac{1}{4} + \dfrac{2}{4} = \dfrac{3}{4}$ *These fractions can be easily added as they already have like denominators.*

Calculator steps: 1 [a^b/c] 4 + 2 [a^b/c] 4 = 3⌐4 = $\dfrac{3}{4}$

or   1 [÷] 4 + 2 [÷] 4 = 0.75   *Since the vinculum in a fraction means division.*

When fractions don't have like denominators, equivalent fractions are used to find them. The like denominator is the *lowest common multiple* of both denominators.

Example

Write the following pair of fractions as equivalent fractions with like denominators: $\dfrac{2}{5}$ and $\dfrac{1}{4}$

Solution

20 is the LCM of 5 and 4.

$\dfrac{2}{5} = \dfrac{x}{20}$; $x = 8$

$\dfrac{1}{4} = \dfrac{x}{20}$; $x = 5$

The two fractions are $\dfrac{8}{20}$ and $\dfrac{5}{20}$.

Example

Evaluate $\frac{1}{4} + \frac{5}{8} + \frac{1}{2}$.

Solution

$\frac{1}{4} + \frac{5}{8} + \frac{1}{2}$ *These fractions have unlike denominators.*

$= \frac{1 \times 2}{4 \times 2} + \frac{5}{8} + \frac{1 \times 4}{2 \times 4}$ *Use equivalent fractions to get a like denominator of 8.*

$= \frac{2}{8} + \frac{5}{8} + \frac{4}{8}$

$= \frac{11}{8}$

$= 1\frac{3}{8}$

Calculator steps: 1 $\boxed{a^b/_c}$ 4 + 5 $\boxed{a^b/_c}$ 8 + 1 $\boxed{a^b/_c}$ 2 = 1 ⌐3 ⌐8 = $1\frac{3}{8}$

or 1 $\boxed{\div}$ 4 + 5 $\boxed{\div}$ 8 + 1 $\boxed{\div}$ 2 = 1.375

Adding and subtracting mixed numbers

When working with fractions approximate the answer first as a check for your exact answer. Often an approximate answer is all that is needed. Find the answer for the whole number part of the question first.

Example

Calculate $2\frac{7}{8} + 3\frac{1}{4}$.

Solution

(a) Approximate: 2 + 3 + more than 1 extra

(since $\frac{7}{8}$ is almost 1) → 6 and something.

(b) Exact calculation:

$2\frac{7}{8} + 3\frac{1}{4}$

$= (2 + 3) + \left(\frac{7}{8} + \frac{1}{4}\right)$

$= 5 + \left(\frac{7}{8} + \frac{1}{4}\right)$

$= 5 + \left(\frac{7}{8} + \frac{1 \times 2}{4 \times 2}\right)$

$= 5 + \left(\frac{7}{8} + \frac{2}{8}\right)$

$= 5 + \frac{9}{8}$ *The fraction $\frac{9}{8}$ is an improper one.*

$= 5 + 1\frac{1}{8}$ *Change it to the mixed number $1\frac{1}{8}$.*

$= 6\frac{1}{8}$

Example

Calculate $5\frac{1}{3} - 2\frac{5}{12}$.

Solution

(a) Approximate: 5 − 2, + or − a bit extra → close to 3.

(b) Exact calculation:

$$5\frac{1}{3} - 2\frac{5}{12}$$
$$= 3 + \left(\frac{1}{3} - \frac{5}{12}\right)$$
$$= 3 + \left(\frac{4}{12} - \frac{5}{12}\right) \quad \frac{4}{12} \text{ is smaller than } \frac{5}{12}. \text{ Split 3 into 2 and } 1 = \frac{12}{12}.$$
$$= 2 + 1 + \left(\frac{4}{12} - \frac{5}{12}\right)$$
$$= 2 + \frac{12}{12} + \left(\frac{4}{12} - \frac{5}{12}\right)$$
$$= 2 + \frac{16}{12} - \frac{5}{12}$$
$$= 2 + \frac{11}{12}$$
$$= 2\frac{11}{12}$$

Calculator steps: 5 $\boxed{a^b/_c}$ 1 $\boxed{a^b/_c}$ 3 − 2 $\boxed{a^b/_c}$ 5 $\boxed{a^b/_c}$ 12 = $2\frac{11}{12}$

or 5 + 1 $\boxed{\div}$ 3 − (2 + 5 $\boxed{\div}$ 12) = 2.916 *The brackets are essential.*

Multiplying fractions

$$\frac{a}{b} \times \frac{c}{d} = \frac{a \times c}{b \times d}$$

Cancel any common factors before multiplying the numerators and denominators together. Factors can be cancelled in any direction except horizontal. Cancel in any of the directions shown:

Example

Calculate $4 \times \frac{7}{12}$.

Solution

$$= \frac{\overset{1}{4}}{1} \times \frac{7}{\underset{3}{\cancel{12}}} \quad 4 \text{ equals } \frac{4}{1}$$
$$= \frac{7}{3}$$
$$= 2\frac{1}{3}$$

Example

Calculate $\frac{7}{8} \times \frac{4}{21}$.

Solution

$$= \frac{\overset{1}{\cancel{7}}}{\underset{2}{\cancel{8}}} \times \frac{\overset{1}{\cancel{4}}}{\underset{3}{\cancel{21}}} \quad \text{Cancel in directions shown above.}$$
$$= \frac{1}{6} \quad \text{Multiply the numerators together, and multiply the denominators together.}$$

Calculator steps: 7 $\boxed{a^b/_c}$ 8 × 4 $\boxed{a^b/_c}$ 21 = 1⌐6 = $\frac{1}{6}$

Mathematics Dictionary **Fractions**

Dividing fractions

To divide by a number is the same as multiplying by its reciprocal.

$$\frac{a}{b} \div \frac{c}{d} = \frac{a}{b} \times \frac{d}{c}$$ *Flip the term after the ÷ sign first.*

Example

Calculate $\frac{1}{3} \div \frac{2}{9}$.

Solution

$\frac{1}{3} \div \frac{2}{9}$ To divide by $\frac{2}{9}$ is the same as multiplying by its reciprocal $\frac{9}{2}$.

$= \frac{1}{\cancel{3}_1} \times \frac{\cancel{9}^3}{2}$ *Turn the question into a multiplication one and proceed as above.*

$= \frac{3}{2}$

$= 1\frac{1}{2}$

Calculator steps: 1 $\boxed{a^b/c}$ 3 ÷ 2 $\boxed{a^b/c}$ 9 = 1⌐1⌐2 = $1\frac{1}{2}$

4 Decimal fractions

A decimal fraction is a number written with a **decimal point**. All decimals except those that are repeating and non-recurring are rational numbers. The number of places in the decimal is the same as the power of 10 (or the number of zeros) in the denominator.

0.6 means 6 parts in 10 or $\frac{6}{10}$.

0.23 means 23 parts in 100 or $\frac{23}{100}$.

A diagram of 0.6, or $\frac{6}{10}$ is:

A diagram of 0.23 or $\frac{23}{100}$ is:

Place value is used to organise decimals as follows:

Wholes				•	Parts		
Thousands	Hundreds	Tens	Units		Tenths	Hundredths	Thousandths
1000	100	10	1		0.1	0.01	0.001

Example

The number $7942.903 = 7000 + 900 + 40 + 2 + 0.9 + 0.003$.
$= 7 \times 1000 + 9 \times 100 + 4 \times 10 + 2 \times 1 + 9 \times 0.1 + 3 \times 0.001$

Comparing the size of decimals

Sizes of decimals are compared one place at a time after the decimal point.

Example

Which is larger—0.6 or 0.23?

Solution

The first numbers after the decimal are 6 and 2. 6 is larger than 2 and so 0.6 is larger than 0.23. This is written as $0.6 > 0.23$.

OPERATIONS INVOLVING DECIMALS

Most decimal questions should be done using the *calculator*. Some ways of completing decimal questions with and without a calculator are given below.

Example

Evaluate 6.72 + 1.8.

Solution

Strategy 1: Adding within each place value
Write the numbers in expanded form and add the numbers in each place value separately.

$$6.72 + 1.8$$
$$= 6 + 0.7 + 0.02 + 1 + 0.8$$
$$= (6 + 1) + (0.7 + 0.8) + 0.02$$
$$= 7 \quad\quad + 1.5 \quad\quad + 0.02$$
$$= 8.5 + 0.02$$
$$= 8.52$$

Strategy 2: Traditional vertical setting out
The numbers are set out one under the other, keeping their place value aligned. Values are added or subtracted within each place value, starting with units.

1. Write the numbers down with place values aligned. Keep decimals under each other.

    6.72
    1.8

2. Add within each decimal place value, starting from the right:
   Hundredths: 2
   Tenths: 7 + 8 = 15 or **5** tenths and 1 unit.

    6.72
    1₁.8
    .52

3. Continue until all places are evaluated.
   Units: 1 + 1 + 6 = **8**

    6.72
    1₁.8
    8.52

MULTIPLYING DECIMALS

Consider the decimal multiplication problem 0.3 × 0.2. This is the same as $\frac{3}{10} \times \frac{2}{10}$ and can be modelled by the following diagram.

$0.3 = \frac{3}{10}$ is represented by the shaded section.

$0.3 \times 0.2 = \frac{3}{10} \times \frac{2}{10}$ is shown by the darker shaded section. There are 6 out of 100 of these squares. $\frac{6}{100} = 0.06$

Hence, 0.3 × 0.2 = 0.06.

Tenths × tenths gives hundredths. Tenths × hundredths gives thousandths and so on.

Example

Calculate the following:
(a) 0.3 × 0.2
(b) 1.002 × 0.2
(c) 3 × 0.002

Solution
(a) 0.3 × 0.2 = 0.06
(b) 1.002 × 0.2 = 0.2004
(c) 3 × 0.002 = 0.006

DIVIDING DECIMALS

To divide by a decimal, multiply the numerator and denominator by the same power of 10 to obtain a whole number in the denominator.

Example

Calculate the following:
(a) $0.3 \div 0.2$ (b) $300 \div 0.02$ (c) $10.48 \div 2$ (d) $0.021 \div 1.4$

Solution

(a) $0.3 \div 0.2$

$= \dfrac{0.3}{0.2}$

$= \dfrac{0.3 \times 10}{0.2 \times 10}$ Multiply both values by 10 to get the whole number 2 in the denominator.

$= \dfrac{3}{2}$

$= 1.5$

(b) $300 \div 0.02$

$= \dfrac{300}{0.02}$

$= \dfrac{300 \times 100}{0.02 \times 100}$ Multiply both values by 100 to get the whole number 2 in the denominator.

$= \dfrac{30\,000}{2}$

$= 15\,000$

(c) Write the numbers in expanded form and divide the numbers in each place value separately.

$10.48 \div 2$
$= (10 + 0.4 + 0.08) \div 2$
$= (10 \div 2) + (0.4 \div 2) + (0.08 \div 2)$
$= 5 \qquad\quad + 0.2 \qquad + 0.04$
$= 5.24$

(d) $0.021 \div 1.4$
$= 0.21 \div 14$ Multiply both values by 10 to get the whole number 14 as the divisor.

Proceed with traditional short division.

1. Write the numbers down with place values aligned. Keep decimals under each other: $14\overline{)0.21}$ with $0.$ above.

2. Divide from the left: $2 \div 14 = 0$ remainder 2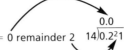

3. Continue until all places are evaluated.
$21 \div 14 = 1$ remainder 7

$14\overline{)0.2^21^70}$ with 0.01 above.

$70 \div 14 = 5$

$14\overline{)0.2^21^70}$ with 0.015 above.

Answer: 0.015

CONVERSION FROM FRACTION TO DECIMAL

Example

Write the following as decimals:

(a) (i) $\frac{6}{10}$ (ii) $\frac{27}{100}$ (iii) $\frac{3}{100}$

(b) $\frac{5}{6}$ (c) $\frac{2}{5}$

Solution

(a) If the denominator of a fraction is a multiple of 10 (e.g. 10, 100, 1000 etc.) the number of zeros in the denominator equals the number of decimal places in the answer.

(i) $\frac{6}{10} = 0.6$ (ii) $\frac{27}{100} = 0.27$ (iii) $\frac{3}{100} = 0.03$

(b) If the denominator is not a multiple of 10, the question can be done by short or long division.

$$\frac{5}{6} = 6\overline{)5.00}^{\,0.83} = 0.83$$

(c) If the denominator is not a multiple of 10, the decimal can more easily be found by using the $\boxed{\div}$ button on your calculator.

$\frac{2}{5} = 0.4$

Calculator steps: 2 $\boxed{\div}$ 5 = 0.4

CONVERSION FROM DECIMAL TO FRACTION

To change from a decimal to a fraction, the number of decimal places is the same as the number of zeros in the denominator. Then reduce to lowest terms.

Example

Write the following as fractions in lowest terms:

(a) 0.55 (b) 0.4 (c) 5.4

Solution

(a) $0.55 = \frac{55}{100}$ There are two decimal places in 0.55 and two zeros in the denominator.

$= \frac{11}{20}$ Reduce to lowest terms.

(b) $0.4 = \frac{4}{10}$ There is one decimal place in 0.4 and one zero in the denominator.

$= \frac{2}{5}$ Reduce to lowest terms

(c) $5.4 = \frac{54}{10}$ There is one decimal place in 5.4 and one zero in the denominator.

$= \frac{27}{5}$ In this case the fraction becomes improper.

$= 5\frac{2}{5}$ Write as a mixed number.

RECURRING DECIMALS

Most of the decimals we have dealt with so far have been **terminating decimals**. A **recurring decimal** occurs when the remainder continues indefinitely. The following are examples of decimals which recur in a pattern.

Example

Write the following as recurring decimals:

(a) $\frac{1}{3}$ (b) $\frac{5}{6}$

Solution

(a) $\frac{1}{3} = 0.333\ 333\ 333\ldots$
    $= 0.\dot{3}$

(b) $\frac{5}{6} = 0.866\ 666\ 666\ldots$
    $= 0.8\dot{6}$ *The dot shows that the digit repeats indefinitely.*
    ≈ 0.87 *Sometimes a dash is used: e.g. $0.8\bar{6}$.*

MULTIPLYING AND DIVIDING BY POWERS OF 10

When **multiplying** by a power of 10, the number is made larger by moving it *left* (←) of the decimal point the same number of places as the power of 10.

When **dividing** by a power of 10, the number is made smaller by moving it *right* (→) of the decimal point the same number of places as the power of 10.

Example

Evaluate the following:

(a) 3.4567×1000 (b) 0.096×10 (c) $3.4567 \div 1000$ (d) $96 \div 10$

Solution

(a) $3.4567 \times 1000 = 3456.7$ *As we are multiplying by 3 powers of ten in 1000, the number is made larger by moving it 3 places left of the decimal point.*

(b) $0.096 \times 10 = 0.96$ *As we are multiplying by 1 power of ten in 10, the number is made larger by moving it 1 place left of the decimal point.*

(c) $3.4567 \div 1000 = 0.003\ 456\ 7$ *As we are dividing by 3 powers of ten in 1000, the number is made smaller by moving it 3 places right of the decimal point.*

(d) $96 \div 10 = 0.96$ *As we are dividing by 2 powers of ten in 100, the number is made smaller by moving it 2 places right of the decimal point.*

IRRATIONAL NUMBERS

Any number that *cannot* be expressed in the form of $\frac{p}{q}$ where p and q are integers and $q \neq 0$ is an irrational number. Some examples of irrational numbers are:
- repeating, non-recurring decimals, such as $3.673\ 045\ 60\ldots\ldots$
- numbers with a square root sign when in their simplified form, such as $\sqrt{2}, \sqrt{31}$.   *Not square roots of numbers which are perfect squares, such as $\sqrt{4}$, since $\sqrt{4} = 2$.*

THE REAL NUMBER SYSTEM

All of the numbers looked at so far make up the **real number system**. This can be represented in a diagram:

Natural numbers
The *natural* or *counting numbers*, not including zero.
Example: 1, 2, 3, 4, 5, 6, . . .

Whole numbers
The *natural numbers* and *zero*.
Example: 0, 1, 2, 3, 4, 5, . . .

Integers
The *positive* and *negative* whole numbers and *zero*.
Example: . . . −4, −3, −2, −1, 0, 1, 2, 3, 4 . . .

Rational numbers
Any number that can be expressed in the form of $\frac{p}{q}$ where p and q are integers and $q \neq 0$.
Example: $\frac{8}{21}$

Irrational numbers
Any number that cannot be expressed in the form of $\frac{p}{q}$ where p and q are integers and $q \neq 0$.
Example: (a) Repeating, non-recurring decimals such as 3.673 045 60 . . .
(b) $\sqrt{2}$, $\sqrt{31}$

Real numbers = Rational numbers + irrational numbers

5 Percentages

THE MEANING OF PER CENT

Per cent means out of 100. The symbol for per cent, a fraction with a denominator of 100: $60\% = \frac{60}{100}$.
In this grid, 60 out of 100 squares are shaded. So, 60% of the grid is shaded.

The percentage of squares not
shaded = 40% or 40 out of 100.
Note: 40% + 60% = 100%.

The following conversions between common fractions, decimals and percentages should be learnt off by heart.

Fraction	Decimal	%	Fraction	Decimal	%
$\frac{1}{2}$	0.5	50%	$\frac{1}{9}$	$0.\overline{1}$	$11\frac{1}{9}\%$
$\frac{1}{3}$	$0.\overline{3}$	$33\frac{1}{3}\%$	$\frac{1}{10}$	0.1	10%
$\frac{2}{3}$	$0.\overline{6}$	$66\frac{2}{3}\%$	$\frac{1}{20}$	0.05	5%
$\frac{1}{4}$	0.25	25%	$\frac{1}{40}$	0.025	$2\frac{1}{2}\%$
$\frac{3}{4}$	0.75	75%	$\frac{1}{50}$	0.02	2%
$\frac{1}{5}$	0.2	20%	$\frac{1}{100}$	0.1	1%
$\frac{1}{8}$	0.125	$12\frac{1}{2}\%$			

LINKING PERCENTAGE, DECIMALS AND FRACTIONS

Conversion from a percentage

- To convert from a percentage to a decimal, divide by 100.
- To convert from a percentage to a fraction, express the percentage as a fraction out of 100 and reduce to lowest terms.

Example

Convert the following to:
    (i)   a decimal and   (ii)   a fraction
(a)   65%   (b)   150%

Solution

(a)   (i)   65%
                  = 65 ÷ 100   *To convert from a percentage to a decimal, divide by 100.*
                  = 0.65
           Calculator steps: 65 ÷ 100 = 0.65

(ii) 65%

$= \dfrac{65}{100}$ *To convert from a percentage to a fraction, express the percentage as a fraction out of 100 and reduce to lowest terms.*

$= \dfrac{13}{20}$

Calculator steps: 65 $\boxed{a^{b}\!/\!c}$ 100 $= 13 \rfloor 20$ *To get the fraction form of the answer you must use the $\boxed{a^{b}\!/\!c}$ button, not the $\div$ button.*

(b) (i) 150%

$= 150 \div 100$ *To convert from a percentage to a decimal, divide by 100.*
$= 1.5$

Calculator steps: 150 $\boxed{\div}$ 100 $= 1.5$

(ii) 150%

$= \dfrac{150}{100}$ *To convert from a percentage to a fraction, express the percentage as a fraction out of 100 and reduce to lowest terms.*

$= \dfrac{3}{2}$

$= 1\dfrac{1}{2}$

Calculator steps: 150 $\boxed{a^{b}\!/\!c}$ 100 $= 1 \rfloor 1 \rfloor 2$

Conversion to a percentage

To convert from a decimal or a fraction to a percentage, multiply by 100 and put in a per cent sign (%).

Example

Convert the following to a percentage:

(a) 0.65   (b) $\dfrac{3}{5}$ (c) $\dfrac{1}{11}$

Solution

(a) 0.65
$= 0.65 \times 100\%$ *Multiply by 100 and put in a per cent sign.*
$= 65\%$
Calculator steps: 0.65 $\boxed{\times}$ 100 $= 65 = 65\%$

(b) $\dfrac{3}{5}$
$= 3 \div 5 \times 100\%$ *Multiply by 100 and put in a per cent sign.*
$= 60\%$
Calculator steps: 3 $\boxed{\div}$ 5 $\times$ 100 $= 60\%$

(c) $\dfrac{1}{11}$

$= \dfrac{1 \times 100}{11}\%$ *Multiply by 100 and put in a per cent sign.*

$= 11 \overline{)100.00}^{\,9.09}$

$= 9.\overline{09}\%$
Calculator steps: 1 $\boxed{\div}$ 11 $\times$ 100 $= 9.\overline{09}\%$

Finding a percentage of a given quantity

$$x\% \text{ of } y = \frac{x \times y}{100}$$

Example

Find 35% of 210.

Solution

$$35\% \text{ of } 210 = \frac{35}{100} \times 210$$

$$= \frac{35}{\underset{2}{\cancel{10}}\cancel{100}} \times \cancel{210}^{21}$$

$$= \frac{7 \times 21}{2}$$

$$= \frac{147}{2}$$

$$= 73.5$$

Example

What percentage of $40 is $24?

Solution

This can be reworded as: Express $24 over $40 as a percentage.

$$\frac{24}{40} \times 100\%$$

$$= 60\%$$

Example

I paid $24 as a 60% deposit. How much did the item cost?

Solution

This can be reworded as: $24 = 60% of what cost?

$$24 = \frac{60}{100} \times x$$

$$24 = 0.6x$$

$$\frac{24}{0.6} = x$$

$$x = \$40$$

PERCENTAGE AND MONEY

Percentages are often used in money transactions. **Commission** is a payment made to a salesperson. It is calculated as a *percentage* of the *value of the goods sold*. A **discount** is a percentage deducted from an original amount.

Example

Thomas earns a commission of 15% on every pair of shoes he sells. Last Saturday he sold $300 worth of shoes. How much did he make?

Solution

$$\text{Commission} = 15\% \text{ of } \$300$$

$$= \frac{15}{100} \times 300$$

$$= \$45$$

Example

B-Mart is having a sale on all jeans. There is a discount of 25% off.
(a) Find the discount on a $95 pair of jeans.
(b) Find the price paid by the customer.

Solution
(a) Discount = 25% of $95
$$= \frac{25}{100} \times 95$$
$$= \$23.75$$
(b) The new price = $95 − discount
$$= \$95 - \$23.75$$
$$= \$71.25$$

Percentage change

$$\text{Percentage change} = \frac{\text{Change}}{\text{First amount}} \times 100\%$$

Example

Goods that were $90 are now selling for $50. What is the percentage change?

Solution
$$\text{Percentage change} = \frac{(90 - 50)}{90} \times 100\%$$
$$= \frac{40}{90} \times 100\%$$
$$= 44\% \text{ reduction}$$

Percentage increase and decrease

Example

Increase the cost of a $1200 refrigerator by 10%.

Solution
Cost of refrigerator becomes: $1200 + 10% of $1200
$$= \$1200 + \frac{10 \times 1200}{100}$$
$$= \$1200 + \$120$$
$$= \$1320$$

Alternative method
Cost of refrigerator becomes: $1200 + 10% of $1200
$$= 100\% \text{ of } \$1200 + 10\% \times \$1200$$
$$= 110\% \text{ of } \$1200$$
$$= \frac{110 \times 1200}{100}$$
$$= \$1320$$

Example

Decrease $30 by $33\frac{1}{3}\%$.

Solution

$$\$30 - 33\tfrac{1}{3}\% \times \$30$$
$$= \$30 - \tfrac{1}{3} \times \$30$$
$$= \$30 - \$10$$
$$= \$20$$

Alternative method

$$\$30 - 33\tfrac{1}{3}\% \times \$30$$
$$= 100\% \times \$30 - 33\tfrac{1}{3}\% \times \$30$$
$$= 66\tfrac{2}{3}\% \times \$30$$
$$= \$20$$

6 Points, lines, angles and plane figures

POINTS AND LINES

- A **point** is a position in space. It has no size.
- A **straight line** is formed by a set of points, all of which obey a particular linear function. It is infinite, having no beginning or end.

    ←———•———————•———→
          A   B   This line is named $\overleftrightarrow{AB}$.

- A **line segment** or interval is the part of the line between two given points.

    A •———————————————• B   This line segment is named $\overline{AB}$.

- A **ray** has a starting point but no end.

    •———————————————→
    A   B   This ray is named $\overrightarrow{AB}$.

- A **horizontal line** is a straight line running in the same direction as, or parallel to, the horizon.

    ←—————————→

- A **vertical line** is a straight line at right angles to the horizontal.

- An **oblique line** is a straight line that lies between the horizontal position and the vertical position.

- When two lines have one point in common, they are said to be **intersecting**.

- When two lines intersect at right angles, they are said to be **perpendicular**.

- **Parallel lines** never meet. Corresponding points on the lines are equal distances apart.

- **Concurrent lines** have a single point of intersection.

- **Coplanar points** lie in the same plane. This is best understood by seeing which lines are not coplanar, such as those marked opposite in a darker shade.

- Two or more points that lie on the same line are **collinear points**.

ANGLES

An angle is the **amount of turn** or **rotation** of a ray. It is measured in **degrees** using a protractor.

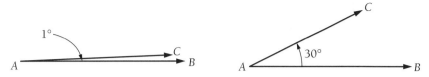

These angles have arms or rays named *AB* and *AC*. The angles are named ∠*CAB* or ∠*BAC*.
Note: An angle is *not* the distance between the two rays.
An angle remains the same regardless of its orientation. The following two angles are both angles of 45°.

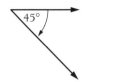

To measure an angle using a protractor, the centre of the protractor is placed directly over one ray, and the position of the other ray gives the degree measure of the angle.

Classification of angles

By 360° rotation

Angles can be classified in relationship to a full rotation of 360°.

- A **full** rotation equals 360°.

- A **three-quarter** rotation equals 270°.

- A **half** rotation equals 180° and is called a straight angle.

- A **quarter** rotation equals 90° and is called a right angle.

By size

- **Acute angle:** angle less than 90°.

- **Obtuse angle:** angle between 90° and 180°.

- **Reflex angle:** angle greater than 180° but less than 360°.

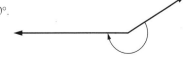

By pairs of angles

- **Complementary angles** add to give 90°: 60° and 30° = 90°.

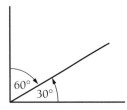

60° and 30° and complementary angles.

- **Supplementary angles** add to give 180°: 120° and 60° = 180°.

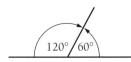

120° and 60° and supplementary angles.

By position

Pairs of angles can be defined in terms of their position with other angles.

- **Vertically opposite angles** are formed when two straight lines intersect.

- **Corresponding angles** form an F shape. *This F is upside down.*

- **Alternate angles** form a Z shape.

- **Cointerior angles** form a U shape.

- **Adjacent angles** are side by side. They share a common arm.

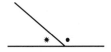

Angle theorems	Code diagram	Example: Find x
Adjacent angles on a straight line are supplementary.		$30° \quad x°$ $30 + x = 180$ $x = 150$
Angles at a point total 360°.		$x°$, $60°$, $70°$, $110°$ $x + 90 + 70 + 110 + 60 = 360$ $x = 30$
Vertically opposite angles are congruent.		$x°$, $130°$ $x = 130$
Corresponding angles on parallel lines are congruent.		$67°$, $x°$ $x = 67$
Cointerior angles on parallel lines are supplementary.		$x°$, $85°$ $x + 85 = 180$ $x = 95$
Alternate angles on parallel lines are congruent.		$x°$, $110°$ $x = 110$

PLANE FIGURES

A **plane figure** is a shape that lies completely within a plane. The shape can be **closed**, which is when all sides meet, or **open**, which is when two sides don't meet. The following are plane figures.

(a) (b) (c) (d) (e)

A **polygon** is a closed plane figure made up of straight line segments. The corners of a polygon are called **vertices**. Each corner is called a **vertex**. Polygons are named for the number of sides they have. Some common polygons are listed below.

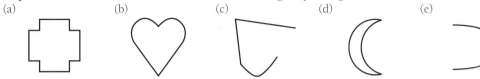

| Triangle | Quadrilateral | Pentagon | Hexagon | Octagon |
| 3 sides | 4 sides | 5 sides | 6 sides | 8 sides |

A **diagonal** is a line that joins two non-adjacent vertices. This pentagon has five diagonals.

A **regular** polygon has equal sides and angles. Some regular polygons are shown below.

regular
pentagon

regular
hexagon

regular
quadrilateral

An **interior angle** of a polygon is an angle inside the shape. An **exterior angle** is formed when one side of the polygon is extended. Interior angles and exterior angle are shown below.

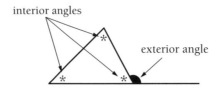

TRIANGLES

Classification of triangles

By size of the angle

- A **right-angled** triangle is one that has a right angle of 90°.

- All angles in an **acute triangle** are acute. They are all less than 90°.

- An **obtuse** triangle has one obtuse angle. One angle is bigger than 90°.

By number of equal sides and angles

- In a **scalene triangle** all angles and sides are different.

- An **isosceles triangle** has two sides and two corresponding angles equal.

- An **equilateral triangle** has all sides and all angles equal.

Triangle theorems	Code diagram	Example: Find x
In an equilateral triangle all sides are equal and all angles equal 60°.		$x = 60$
In an isosceles triangle, angles opposite the equal sides are equal.		$x = 75$
The exterior angle of a triangle equals the sum of the two interior opposite angles.		$x = 55 + 70$ $x = 125$
The sum of the angles of a triangle is 180°.		$x + 80 + 60 = 180$ $x = 40$

QUADRILATERALS

There are many different kinds of quadrilaterals, which are defined by their angles and sides:
- A **quadrilateral** is a four-sided closed figure.

- A **trapezium** is a quadrilateral in which two sides are parallel.  or

- A **parallelogram** is a quadrilateral in which both pairs of opposite sides are parallel.

- A **rectangle** is a parallelogram in which all angles are right angles.

- A **rhombus** is a parallelogram in which all sides are equal.

- A **square** is a rectangle in which all sides are equal.

- A **kite** is a quadrilateral in which two pairs of adjacent sides are equal. *Adjacent sides have a common vertex.*

Mathematics Dictionary Points, lines, angles and plane figures

Quadrilateral theorems	Code diagram	Example: Find x
The sum of the angles of a quadrilateral is 360°.		$x + 50 + 100 + 90 = 360°$ $x = 120°$
The opposite angles of a parallelogram are equal.		$x = 80$

CIRCLES

A special plane figure is called a circle. A **circle** is a closed curve in which the centre is equidistant from every point on the curve. A circle can be drawn with a **compass**.

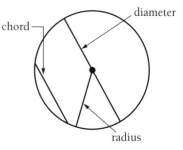

- A **chord** is a line joining any two points on a circle.
- The **circumference** is the distance around the outside of a circle.
- A **diameter** is a chord that passes through the centre of the circle.
- The **radius** of a circle is a line from the centre of the circle to any point on the circumference.

- Any part of the circumference of a circle is called an **arc**. If an arc is larger than half the circumference, it is called a **major arc**. If it is smaller than half, it is called a **minor arc**.

- A chord divides a circle into a **major segment** and a **minor segment**.

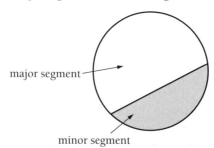

- An exact **half circle** is called a semicircle.

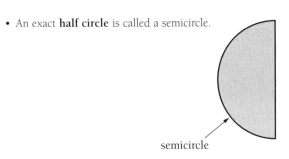
semicircle

- Two radii divide a circle into a **major sector** and a **minor sector**.

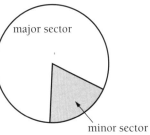
major sector

minor sector

- A sector that is one-quarter of a circle is called a **quadrant**.

 quadrant

concentric circles

- **Concentric circles** have the same centre point but their radii are different in length.

- A circle with a concentric circle removed from its centre is called an **annulus**.

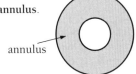
annulus

- Another shape with a curved edge is the **ellipse**. An ellipse looks like a flattened or elongated circle. An ellipse is different from an oval in that an oval is egg-shaped and bigger at one end than the other.

- A **cyclic quadrilateral** is one in which all vertices contact with the circle circumference.
- A **central angle** is an angle with its vertex at the centre of the circle and its rays contacting the circumference.
- A circle has **360°**.

SYMMETRY

A shape is **symmetrical** if one half can be reflected exactly on to the other half. The line of reflection is called the **axis of symmetry**. These figures are symmetrical.

Mathematics Dictionary   Points, lines, angles and plane figures

Mathematics Dictionary Points, lines, angles and plane figures

Circle theorems	Coded diagram	Example: Find x
A **tangent** to a circle is perpendicular to the radius drawn at the point of contact. A tangent is a line that touches the circle in one place only.		$x = 90$
The central angle is double the angle at the circumference standing on the same arc.		$x = 55$
Angles at the circumference that stand on the same arc are congruent.		$x = 75$.
The angle in a semicircle is a right angle.		$x = 90$
The opposite angles of a cyclic quadrilateral are supplementary.		$x + 95 = 180$ $x = 85$
A line from the centre of a circle and perpendicular to a chord bisects that chord.		$x = 5$
The exterior angle of a cyclic quadrilateral is congruent to the interior opposite angle.		$x = 100$
Tangents drawn to a circle from an external point are congruent.		$x = 15$
The length of an arc is proportional to its central angle.	Arc length $= \frac{a}{360} \times 2\pi r$	Find the length of the minor arc. The radius of the circle = 7 cm. Arc length $= \frac{100}{360} \times 2 \times \pi \times 7$ $x = 12.22$

Some figures have more than one axis of symmetry.
This shape has two:

This shape has four:

A shape has **rotational symmetry** if it can be rotated about a point, called its **centre of symmetry**, and get exactly the same shape *more than once in a 360° rotation*.
This shape has rotational symmetry about the point indicated. If we put a pin on this point and rotate the shape through 60°, 120°, 180°, 240° or 300°, we get exactly the *same* shape the same way around.

This shape, however, does not have rotational symmetry about any point. We cannot rotate the shape through any angle and get exactly the same shape the same way around.

Example

Show that this shape has rotational symmetry about the point indicated.

Solution

1. Copy the shape using tracing paper, cut it out and place a pin at its centre. Place the traced shape over the top of the original. *The pin is to keep the centre of the shape steady.*

2. Rotate the shape and see if you get exactly the same shape before you reach a complete turn. This shape does so five times—at 60°, 120°, 180°, 240° and 300° turns.

90° or quarter turn   135° turn   60°, 120°, 180°, 240° and 300° turns

No   No   Yes

Hence, the shape does have rotational symmetry.

7 Algebra

Algebra is the study of patterns of numbers.

ALGEBRAIC TERMINOLOGY

Algebraic expressions are categorised as either sums, differences, products or quotients.

An algebraic expression is a sum when addition is the last operation to be performed. Even a difference can be considered as a sum. For example: $x - y = x + -y$.

An algebraic expression is a product when multiplication is the last operation to be performed. Even a quotient can be considered as a product. For example: $\frac{x}{y} = x \times \frac{1}{y}$.

Sums
In the expression $3x + 5$:
- there are two **terms**—$3x$ and 5
- the **variable** is x
- the **constant term** is the term without a variable—in this case 5
- the **coefficient** is the value in front of the variable—in this case 3
- this expression is a **sum** as the last operation to be performed is addition

Differences
In the expression $x - y$:
- the **variables** are x and y
- the **constant** term is 0, since $x - y = x - y + 0$
- the **coefficient** of x is 1 and the coefficient of y is -1
- this expression is a **difference** as the last operation to be performed is subtraction

Products
In the expression $2xy$:
- there are three factors—2, x and y
- the **variables** are x and y
- the **coefficient** is the value in front of the variable—in this case 2
- this expression is a **product** as the last operation to be performed is multiplication

Note: In algebraic expressions the $\times$ sign is left out between two factors (unless they are both numbers). The computer uses * to mean multiply.

Quotients
In the expression $\frac{a}{2b}$:
- the **variables** are a and b
- the **coefficient** of a is 1 and the coefficient of b is 2
- This expression is a **quotient** as the last operation to be performed is division

Example

Simplify $2 \times 3 \times x \times y$.

Solution

$2 \times 3 \times x \times y = 6xy$

Example

For the following expressions:
  (i) name the variables, constant term and coefficient
  (ii) define the expression as a sum, difference, product or quotient and name the terms or factors

  (a) $4x + 3y - 8$
  (b) $4xy$
  (c) $\dfrac{-2}{a}$

Solution
  (a) (i) x and y are both variables; the coefficient of x is 4 and the coefficient of y is 3. The constant term is –8.
      (ii) This expression is a sum with three terms—$4x$, $3y$ and –8.
  (b) (i) x and y are both variables; the coefficient is 4.
      (ii) This expression is a product with three factors—4, x and y.
  (c) (i) a is the variable; the coefficient is –2.
      (ii) This expression is a quotient with two factors— –2 and $\dfrac{1}{a}$.

POWER NOTATION

Algebraic expressions use power notation when there is a repetition of equal factors. The expression $4 \times x \times x \times x \times x$ is written as $4x^3$. The notation for this expression is:
- $4x^3$ is the **power**
- 4 is the **coefficient**
- x is the **base**
- 3 is the **index** or **exponent**

Example

Write the following expression using power notation:
$8 \times y \times y \times y \times x \times x$

Solution
This expression in power notation is: $8y^3x^2$

Example

Write the following expressions in expanded form and name their coefficient, base and index:
  (a) $3y^5$
  (b) x

Solution
  (a) $3y^5 = 3 \times y \times y \times y \times y \times y$ 3 is the coefficient, y is the base, 5 is the index or exponent.
  (b) x is already expanded as there is only one factor $x = 1 \times x^1$ and so 1 is the coefficient, x is the base and 1 is the index or exponent.

Example

Write the expression $(4y)^3$ in expanded form and simplify.

Solution
Because there is a bracket around the $4y$ this is repeated three times.
$(4y)^3 = 4y \times 4y \times 4y$
$= 64y^3$

ALGEBRA AND THE FOUR OPERATIONS

Like terms are terms with the **same variable**. The like terms in $2x$, $2y$, $-5x$ and $6y$ are: $2x$ and $-5x$, and $2y$ and $6y$.

Example

In the following lists, which are the like terms?
(a) $a, 2b, 5a, 3, 9$
(b) $7ac, 8ab, 10b, abc, 3ac, -2ba, 5abc$

Solution
(a)   The following are like terms:
a and $5a$
3 and 9
(b)   The following are like terms:
$7ac$ and $3ac$
$8ab$ and $-2ba$
abc and $5abc$ Note: *abc is the same as acb and bca and bac and so on.*

Adding and subtracting like terms

Like terms can be added or subtracted.

Example

Simplify the following, using diagrams to explain your answer. $= a$ $= b$ ● $= 1$
(a) $a + 2a$
(b) $2a + 1$
(c) $a + 3 + b + 2$
(d) $a + 2 + b + 1 + 3b + 2a$

Solution
(a) $a + 2a = 3a$ *a is the same as 1a; 2a and a are like terms and can be added.*

(b) $= 2a + 1$ *No further simplification possible as 2a and 1 are not like terms and cannot be added.*

(c) $a + 3 + b + 2 = a + b + 5$ *a and b cannot be added as they are not like terms.*

(d) $a + 2 + b + 1 + 3b + 2a$
$= 3a + 4b + 3$ *First add the terms in a, then the terms in b, and then the constant terms.*

Example

Simplify without diagrams:
(a) $2a - a$
(b) $2abc - 6acb$
(c) $2xy + 3x + 5xy + 4x$
(d) $14x^2y - 8yx^2 + 3$

Solution
(a) $2a - a$
$= a$ $-a$ *is the same as* $-1a$
(b) $2abc - 6acb$
$= -4abc$ *abc and acb are equal*
(c) $2xy + 3x + 5xy + 4x$
$= 7xy + 7x$
(d) $14x^2y - 8yx^2 + 3$
$= 6x^2y + 3$

Multiplying and dividing algebraic expressions

When multiplying and dividing algebraic expressions, note the following:
- × signs are left out
- variable combinations are written using power notation where possible
- constants are multiplied together
- constants divided may be cancelled to lowest terms
- beware of rules for negatives, such as $- \times -$ gives a positive

Example

Simplify the following expressions:
(a) $4x \times 5y$
(b) $3x \times 7x$
(c) $(-3xy)^2$
(d) $\dfrac{8x}{4y}$

Solution

(a) $4x \times 5y$
$= 20xy$ *Remember it is common to leave out the × sign between two factors, unless they are both numbers.*

(b) $3x \times 7x$
$= 21x^2$ $x \times x = x^2$

(c) $(-3xy)^2$
$= -3xy \times -3xy$
$= 9x^2y^2$

(d) $\dfrac{8x}{4y}$

$= \dfrac{{}^2 8x}{{}_1 4y}$

$= \dfrac{2x}{y}$

THE DISTRIBUTIVE LAW

We use the **distributive law** for multiplication in algebraic expressions.
For example, the expression $4(y + 3)$ can be simplified in a diagram.
Let each rectangle represent the variable y.
Let each square represent one 1.

The grouping opposite shows
4 lots of $y + 3$, that is $4(y + 3)$.

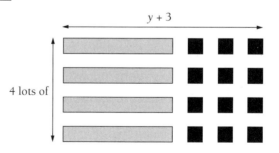

4 lots of

By counting the shapes, we can see that $4(y + 3)$ also equals $4y + 12$. Hence, $4(y + 3) = 4y + 12$.

The distributive law states that:
$$a(b + c) = a \times b + a \times c$$
$$\text{or } a \times b + a \times c = a(b + c)$$

Mathematics Dictionary **Algebra**

Expanding algebraic expressions

Using the distributive law

Expanding algebraic expressions using the distributive law turns a product into a sum. The rule is used in this form:
$$a(b + c) = a \times b + a \times c$$
The value outside the bracket is multiplied by everything inside the bracket.

Example

Expand the following using the distributive law.
(a) $3(4x - 5)$ (b) $-c(2a + 5)$
(c) $-(-8 + 2a)$ (d) $4(2a - 1) + 2a$

Solution

(a) $3(4x - 5)$
$= 12x - 15$ *3 is multiplied by both the 4x and the −5*

(b) $-c(2a + 5)$
$= -2ac - 5$ *Take note that the − gets multiplied as well as the c.*

(c) $-(-8 + 2a)$
Change this to: $-1(-8 + 2a)$
$= 8 + -2a$

(d) $4(2a - 1) + 2a$
$= 10a - 4$ *Note that the 4 is only multiplied by the terms in the bracket, not the 2a.*

With the pattern (a + b)(c + d):

$$(a + b)(c + d) = ac + bc + ad + bd$$ *Every term in the first bracket is multiplied by every term in the second bracket.*

Sometimes this is remembered as FOIL: F = first × first
O = outside × outside
I = inside × inside
L = last × last

Example

Expand $(a - 5)(a + 8)$.

Solution

$(a - 5)(a + 8)$
$= a^2 + 8a - 5a - 40$
$= a^2 + 3a - 40$

Example

Expand $4(a - 5)(a + 8)$.

Solution

$4(a - 5)(a + 8)$
$= (4a - 20)(a + 8)$ *(Note: The 4 is multiplied through one bracket only.)*
$= 4a^2 + 32a - 20a - 160$
$= 4a^2 + 12a - 160$

With the patterns (a + b)² and (a − b)²

$$(a + b)^2 = a^2 + 2ab + b^2 \quad (a - b)^2 = a^2 - 2ab + b^2$$

Example

Expand $(2a + 7)^2$

Solution

$(2a + 7)^2$
$= (2a)^2 + 2 \times 2a \times 7 + 7^2$
$= 4a^2 + 28a + 49$

Example

Expand $(ab - 3)^2$

Solution

$(ab)^2 - 2 \times ab \times 3 + 3^2$
$= a^2b^2 - 6ab + 9$

Expressions with more terms

The FOIL rule only applies when a bracket with two terms is multiplied by another bracket with two terms. When there are more than two terms in a bracket, proceed as follows.

Example

Expand $(x + 4)(x^2 + 2x - 1)$

Solution

$(x + 4)(x^2 + 2x - 1)$
$= x(x^2 + 2x - 1) + 4(x^2 + 2x - 1)$ *Multiply the first term by everything in the second bracket. Then multiply the second term by everything in the second bracket.*

$= x^3 + 2x^2 - x + 4x^2 + 8x - 4$
$= x^3 + 6x^2 + 7x - 4$ *Collect like terms.*

FACTORISING

When factorising simple algebraic expressions, try the following techniques in the order given:
1. Try the distributive law, looking for a common factor.
2. Look for a pattern—the difference between two squares, the difference or sum of two cubes.
3. Check if the expression is a trinomial.

Using the distributive law

Factorising using the distributive law turns a sum into a product. The rule used in this form is:
$a \times b + a \times c = a(b + c)$ *The common factor is taken outside the bracket.*

Example

Factorise the following using the distributive law:
(a) $6x + 4$ (b) $-4x - 2$ (c) $6xy - 4xz$

Solution

(a) $6x + 4 = 2(3x + 2)$ *The factor common to each term is 2.*
(b) $-4x - 2 = -2(2x + 1)$ *If both terms are negative, put the negative outside the bracket.*
(c) $6xy - 4xz = 2x(3y - 2z)$ *Always factorise fully by taking out everything that is common—both the x and the 2 are common.*

Trickier factorising

Example

Factorise the following:
(a) $-15x^2 + 20x$ (b) $7x(x - 1) + 5(x - 1)$ (c) $16xy - 4x^2y + 20x$

Solution

(a) $-15x^2 + 20x$
$= -5x(3x - 4)$ When the first term is negative, make the **outside factor** negative.

(b) $7x(x - 1) + 5(x - 1)$
$= (x - 1)(7x + 5)$ Sometimes the **common factor** is itself in a bracket.

(c) $16xy - 4x^2y + 20x$
$= 4x(4y - xy + 5)$ The common factors must be in **all** terms.

Factorising with patterns

The difference between two squares

$$a^2 - b^2 = (a + b)(a - b)$$

Example

Factorise $a^2 - 16$.

Solution

$a^2 - 16$
$= (a - 4)(a + 4)$

Example

Factorise $3s^2 - 12b^2$.

Solution

$3s^2 - 12b^2$
$= 3(s^2 - 4b^2)$ Here the distributive law is applied first.
$= 3(s - 2b)(s + 2b)$

Example

Factorise $16x^4 - 1$.

Solution

$16x^4 - 1$
$= (4x^2 + 1)(4x^2 - 1)$ The second factor is itself a difference between two squares.
$= (4x^2 + 1)(2x + 1)(2x - 1)$

The difference between two cubes

$$a^3 - b^3 = (a - b)(a^2 + ab + b^2)$$

Example

Factorise $a^3 - 48$.

Solution

$a^3 - 48$
$= (a - 4)(a^2 + 4a + 12)$

The sum of two cubes

$$a^3 + b^3 = (a + b)(a^2 - ab + b^2)$$

Example

Factorise $27s^3 + 216a^3b^3$.

Solution

$27s^3 + 216a^3b^3$
$= (3s + 6ab)(9s^2 - 18sab + 36a^2b^2)$

Factorising a trinomial

A trinomial takes the form of $ax^2 + bx + c$.
1. Name a—the coefficient of x^2; name b—the coefficient of x; name c—the constant term.
2. Draw a table to find factors of $a \times c$ to give b.
3. Use these factors to break up the term in x, then group the first two and last two terms.
4. Apply the distributive law to each bracket in turn, taking out the common factor.
5. Apply the distributive law, using the common bracket as a common factor.

Example

Factorise $x^2 - 7x + 12$.

Solution

$a = 1; b = -7; c = 12$ *Think: Find factors of ac to give b.*

$x^2 - 7x + 12$
$= (x^2 - 4x) + (-3x + 12)$ *step 3*
$= x(x - 4) + -3(x - 4)$ *step 4*
$= (x - 3)(x - 4)$ *step 5*

Factors of ac = 12	Sum to give b = −7	
12, 1	12 + 1 = 13	No
2, 6	2 + 6 = 8	No
3, 4	3 + 4 = 7	No
−3, −4	−3 + −4 = −7	Yes. So replace the term −7x by −3x and −4x.

Example

Factorise $-3x + -5 + 2x^2$.

Solution

$a = 2; b = -3; c = -5$ *Note that a is still the value in front of x^2 even though it is the last term.*

$2x^2 + -3x + -5$
$= (2x^2 + -5x) + (2x + -5)$
$= x(2x + -5) + 1(2x + -5)$
$= (x + 1)(2x + -5)$

Factors of ac = −10	Sum to give b = −3	
10, −1	10 + −1 = 9	No
5, −2	5 + −2 = 3	No
−5, 2	−5 + 2 = −3	Yes. Replace the term −3x by −5x and 2x.

SUBSTITUTION

To substitute into an algebraic expression is to replace the variables with the values given.

Example

Evaluate $a + 2$ when $a = 3$.

Solution

$a + 2$
$= 3 + 2$ *The variable a is replaced by the value 3.*
$= 5$

Example

Evaluate $\frac{a-b}{2b}$ when $a = -1$ and $b = -5$.

Solution

$$\frac{a-b}{2b}$$

$$= \frac{-1 - -5}{2 \times -5} \quad \text{Care is needed with negatives.}$$

$$= \frac{-1 + 5}{-10}$$

$$= \frac{4}{-10}$$

$$= -\frac{2}{5} \quad \text{The expression is evaluated with the new values.}$$

ALGEBRAIC SIMPLIFICATION OF RATIONAL EXPRESSIONS

Adding and subtracting rational expressions

The same rules as those used to add and subtract fractions are used to add and subtract rational algebraic expressions. When we add and subtract fractions, we find like denominators, that is, the lowest common multiple of both denominators.

Example

Find the lowest common denominator for the following algebraic expressions: $\frac{3}{4x}$ and $-\frac{5c}{2p}$

Solution
1. First choose all the factors of the first denominator: 4 and x.
2. Next choose any factors of the second denominator that have not already been chosen: p has not yet been chosen and 2 is already a factor of 4. The LCM is $4 \times x \times p = 4xp$.

Example

Simplify $\frac{3}{4x} - \frac{5c}{2p}$.

Solution

$$\frac{3}{4x} - \frac{5c}{2p}$$

$$= \frac{3}{4x} + \frac{-5c}{2p} \quad \text{Put the negative close to the 5c to avoid confusion.}$$

$$\frac{3 \times p}{4x \times p} + \frac{-5c \times 2x}{2p \times 2x} \quad \text{In the previous example, the LCM of 4xp was found. Make the fractions equivalent.}$$

$$= \frac{3p + -10cx}{4xp} \quad \text{The fractions have like denominators and can be added.}$$

Example

Simplify $5 + \frac{7}{x-1}$.

Solution

$$5 + \frac{7}{x-1}$$

$$= \frac{5}{1} + \frac{7}{1(x-1)} \quad \text{Use a bracket for } (x-1) \text{ to make the factors clear—1 and } x-1.$$

$$= \frac{5(x-1)}{1(x-1)} + \frac{7}{1(x-1)} \quad \text{The LCM is } 1(x-1). \text{ Make equivalent fractions.}$$

$$= \frac{5x - 5 + 7}{(x - 1)} \quad \text{Expand brackets at the same time as adding the rationals.}$$

$$= \frac{5x + 2}{(x - 1)} \quad \text{Collect like terms.}$$

Multiplying and dividing rational expressions

As with multiplying and dividing fractions, like denominators are not needed to multiply and divide rational expressions.

Example

Simplify $\frac{3p^2}{4x} \times \frac{2c}{p}$.

Solution

$$\frac{3p^2}{4x} \times \frac{2c}{p}$$

$$= \frac{3pp}{4x} \times \frac{2c}{p} \quad \text{Write } p^2 \text{ as } p \times p \text{ to see common factors more clearly.}$$

$$= \frac{3\cancel{p}p}{{}_2\cancel{4}x} \times \frac{\cancel{2}c}{\cancel{p}} \quad \text{Cancel common factors.}$$

$$= \frac{3pc}{2x} \quad \text{Multiply remaining denominators together and numerators together.}$$

Example

Simplify $\frac{27(k - 1)}{5p^2} \div \frac{9(k - 1)^2}{10p}$.

$$\frac{27(k - 1)}{5p^2} \div \frac{9(k - 1)^2}{10p} \quad \text{Flip first and cancel.}$$

$$= \frac{{}^3\cancel{27}(k - 1)^1}{\cancel{5}p} \times \frac{{}^2\cancel{10}\cancel{p}}{{}_1\cancel{9}(k - 1)}$$

$$= \frac{6}{p(k - 1)}$$

Simplifying rational expressions involving factorisation

Example

Simplify $\frac{x^2 - 7x + 12}{x^2 - x - 6}$.

Solution

$$\frac{x^2 - 7x + 12}{x^2 - x - 6}$$

$$= \frac{(x - 3)(x - 4)}{(x - 3)(x + 2)} \quad \text{First factorise the trinomals.}$$

$$= \frac{x - 4}{x + 2} \quad \text{Cancel common factors.}$$

Example

Add and simplify $\dfrac{2x}{x^2 - x - 6} + \dfrac{3x}{x^2 + x - 12}$.

Solution

$\dfrac{2x}{x^2 - x - 6} + \dfrac{3x}{x^2 + x - 12}$ Factorise denominators.

$= \dfrac{2x}{(x - 3)(x + 2)} + \dfrac{3x}{(x - 3)(x + 4)}$ The **vinculum** is the line that separates the numerator and denominator. It means to bracket everything over and under the line and divide.

$= \dfrac{2x(x + 4)}{(x - 3)(x + 2)(x + 4)} + \dfrac{3x(x + 2)}{(x - 3)(x + 4)(x + 2)}$ Find the LCM and hence equivalent fractions. The LCM is $(x - 3)(x + 2)(x + 4)$.

$= \dfrac{2x^2 + 8x + 3x^2 + 6x}{(x - 3)(x + 2)(x + 4)}$ Expand the numerators as the fractions are added.

$= \dfrac{5x^2 + 14x}{(x - 3)(x + 2)(x + 4)}$ Factorise the numerator to check for factors that can cancel.

$= \dfrac{x(5x + 14)}{(x - 3)(x + 2)(x + 4)}$ No more common factors.

8 Solving linear equations

An **equation** is a mathematical statement where two quantities are equal. For example: $2x + 1 = 10$ or $3x + 4 = 5x + 7$.

INVERSE OPERATIONS

When solving **linear equations**, we find the unknown variable. To do this we perform the same operation on both sides of the equation by using **inverse operations**. The inverse operation of addition is subtraction. The inverse operation of multiplication is division.

Example

Solve the equation $x + 5 = 9$.

Solution

$x + 5 = 9$
$x + 5 - 5 = 9 - 5$ The opposite of adding 5 is to subtract 5. Do the same to both sides.
$x + 0 = 4$ Simplify any operations possible. Here $5 - 5 = 0$ and $9 - 5 = 4$.
$x = 4$ The equation is solved.

Example

Solve the equation $x - 3 = 7$.

Solution

$x - 3 = 7$
$x - 3 + 3 = 7 + 3$ The opposite of subtracting 3 is to add 3. Do the same to both sides.
$x + 0 = 10$ Simplify any operations possible. Here $-3 + 3 = 0$, and $7 + 3 = 10$.
$x = 10$ The equation is solved.

Example

Solve the equation $2y = 8$.

Solution

$2y = 8$

$\dfrac{2y}{2} = \dfrac{8}{2}$ or $2y \div 2 = 8 \div 2$ The opposite of multiplying by 2 is dividing by 2. Do the same to both sides.

$\dfrac{\cancel{2}^1 y}{\cancel{2}_1} = \dfrac{\cancel{8}^4}{\cancel{2}_1}$ Simplify any operations possible. Here $\dfrac{2}{2} = 1$ and $\dfrac{8}{2} = 4$.

$y = 4$ Dividing by 2 is the same as multiplying by $\dfrac{1}{2}$.

Example

Solve the equation $t \div 3 = 4$.

Solution

$t \div 3 = 4$

$t \div 3 \times 3 = 4 \times 3$ or $\dfrac{t}{3} \times 3 = 4 \times 3$ The opposite of dividing by 3 is to multiply by 3. Do the same to both sides.

$t = 12$ Simplify. Here $\dfrac{3}{3} = 1$ and $4 \times 3 = 12$.

Example

Solve the equation $\frac{2}{3}z = 8$.

Solution

$$\frac{2}{3}z = 8$$

$(\frac{3}{2} \times \frac{2}{3})z = \frac{3}{2} \times 8$ *The opposite of multiplying by $\frac{2}{3}$ is to multiply by its reciprocal $\frac{3}{2}$.*

$1 \times z = 12$ *Simplify. Here $\frac{3}{2} \times \frac{2}{3} = 1$ and $\frac{3}{\cancel{2}} \times \cancel{8}^4 = 12$.*

$z = 12$

Order in equations with more steps

Some equations involve more steps to find the variable of these steps.
- Do inverse operations of + and − first.
- Then do inverse operations of × and ÷.

This procedure is called **backtracking**.

Example

Solve the equations

(a) $2x - 5 = 7$ (b) $\frac{r}{-5} + 1 = 2$ (c) $8 - 4p = 7$

Solution

(a)
$2x - 5 = 7$
$2x - 5 + 5 = 7 + 5$ *Do the inverse operation of − first. The opposite of subtracting 5 is adding 5.*
$2x = 12$ *Simplify. Here $-5 + 5 = 0$ and $7 + 5 = 12$.*
$\frac{2x}{2} = \frac{12}{2}$ *Do the inverse operation of × next. The opposite of multiplying by 2 is to divide by 2.*
$x = 6$ *Simplify. Here $\frac{2}{2} = 1$ and $\frac{12}{2} = 6$.*

(b) $\frac{r}{-5} + 1 = 2$

$\frac{r}{-5} + 1 - 1 = 2 - 1$ *Do the inverse operation of + first. The opposite of adding 1 is to subtract 1.*

$\frac{r}{-5} = 1$ *Simplify. Here $1 - 1 = 0$ and $2 - 1 = 1$.*

$\frac{r}{-5} \times -5 = 1 \times -5$ *Do the inverse operation of ÷ next. The opposite of dividing by −5 is to multiply by −5.*

$r = -5$ *Simplify. Here $\frac{-5}{-5} = 1$ and $1 \times -5 = -5$.*

(c) $8 - 4p = 7$
$-4p + 8 = 7$ *When there is a negative in front of the variable, rewrite the equation with the negative term first.*
$-4p + 8 - 8 = 7 - 8$ *Proceed as for other examples.*
$-4p = -1$
$\frac{-4p}{-4} = \frac{-1}{-4}$
$p = \frac{1}{4}$

Equations with brackets

When an equation has brackets, two approaches are used.
1. When the number outside the bracket is a whole number, expand the brackets using the distributive law first.

Example

Solve the equation $3(w + 6) = 9$.

Solution
$$3(w + 6) = 9$$
$$3w + 18 = 9$$
$$3w + 18 + -18 = 9 + -18$$
$$3w = -9$$
$$\frac{3w}{3} = \frac{-9}{3}$$
$$w = -3$$

2. When the number outside the bracket is a **fraction**, multiply both sides by its reciprocal and cancel.

Example

Solve the equation $\frac{2}{3}(2x - 1) = -4$.

Solution
$$\frac{2}{3}(2x - 1) = -4$$
$$\frac{3}{2} \times \frac{2}{3}(2x + -1) = \frac{3}{2} \times -4$$
$$2x + -1 = -6$$
$$2x + -1 + 1 = -6 + 1$$
$$2x = -5$$
$$\frac{2x}{2} = \frac{-5}{2}$$
$$x = -\frac{5}{2}$$

Solving equations that involve collecting variables

When solving an equation where the variable appears more than once, collect the variables on one side first.

Example

Solve the following equations: (a) $3(p - 1) + p = 7$ (b) $3(x - 2) = x + 8$.

Solution

(a) $3(p - 1) + p = 7$
    $3p - 3 + p = 7$ *Expand the brackets first using the distributive law.*
    $4p - 3 = 7$ *Collect the like terms.*
    $4p = 10$ *Add 3 to both sides.*
    $p = \frac{5}{2}$ *Proceed as for other question.*

(b) $3(x - 2) = x + 8$ *Expand the brackets first.*
    $3x - 6 = x + 8$ *Put both variables on the same side of the = sign by subtracting x from both sides.*
    $2x - 6 = 8$
    $2x = 14$ *Evaluate.*
    $x = 7$

Equations involving rational numbers

Remember that the *vinculum* means to bracket everything over and under the line and divide. Hence, $\frac{3a+7}{4}$ is the same as $\frac{(3a+7)}{4}$.

Example

Solve the equation $2a - 4 = \frac{3a+7}{4}$.

Solution

$$2a - 4 = \frac{3a+7}{4}$$

$(2a - 4) \times 4 = \frac{(3a+7)}{4} \times 4$ Multiply both sides by the lowest common denominator. Here it is 4.

$8a - 16 = 3a + 7$ Expand and cancel.
$8a - 16 - 3a = 3a - 3a + 7$ Put all the variables on the same side of the = sign.
$8a - 3a - 16 = 0 + 7$
$5a - 16 = 7$ Solve.
$5a = 23$
$a = \frac{23}{5}$

Example

Solve the equation $\frac{3a-4}{5} = \frac{7-4a}{3}$.

Solution

$$\frac{3a-4}{5} = \frac{7-4a}{3}$$ The LCM of 5 and 3 is 15.

$\left(\frac{3a-4}{5}\right) \times 15^3 = \left(\frac{7-4a}{3}\right) \times 15^5$ The vinculum implies brackets.

$3(3a - 4) = 5(7 - 4a)$ Expand and cancel.
$9a - 12 = 35 - 20a$
$9a + 20a - 12 = 35 - 20a + 20a$ Put all the variables on the same side of the = sign.
$29a = 35 + 12$
$29a = 47$
$a = \frac{47}{29}$
$a = 1.62$

Example

Solve the equation $\frac{5a-1}{6} = \frac{3-a}{7} + 1$.

Solution

$$\frac{5a-1}{6} = \frac{3-a}{7} + 1$$

$\frac{5a-1}{6} = \frac{3-a}{7} + \frac{1}{1}$ The LCM of 6, 7 and 1 is 42.

$\left(\frac{5a-1}{6}\right) \times 42^7 = \left(\frac{3-a}{7}\right) \times 42^6 + \frac{42}{1}$ The vinculum implies brackets. Everything is multiplied by the 42, including the 1. Cancel.

$7(5a - 1) = 6(3 - a) + 42$

$$35a - 7 = 18 - 6a + 42 \quad \text{Expand.}$$
$$35a - 7 + 6a = 60 - 6a + 6a \quad \text{Put all the variables on the same side of the = sign.}$$
$$41a - 7 = 60 + 0 \quad \text{Solve.}$$
$$41a = 67$$
$$a = 1.63$$

INEQUATIONS

An **inequation** is a mathematical statement where two quantities are not necessarily equal. Linear inequalities are written with the signs $<, \leq, >$ and $\geq$.

- $<$ means is less than
- $\leq$ means is less than or equal to
- $>$ means is greater than
- $\geq$ means is greater than or equal to

The following inequations are solved using a number line.

Example

Show the solution to $x \leq 7$ on a number line.

Solution

The direction for less than is to the left ($\leftarrow$).

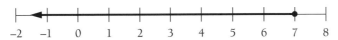

When the sign includes 'or is equal to' ($\leq$), the dot on the end of the ray is coloured in. This means that 7 is included in the solution.

Example

Show the solution to $x < -2$ on a number line.

Solution

The direction for less than is to the left ($\leftarrow$).

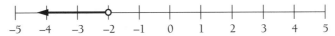

When the sign does not include 'or is equal to' ($<$), the dot on the end of the ray is open. This means that -2 is not included in the solution.

Example

Show the solution to $x \geq -1$ on a number line.

Solution

The direction for greater than is to the right ($\rightarrow$).

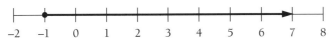

This sign includes 'or is equal to' and so the dot on the end of the ray is coloured in. The -1 is included in the solution.

Example

Show the solution to $x > 3$ on a number line.

Solution

The direction for greater than is to the right ($\rightarrow$).

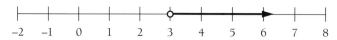

This sign does not include 'or equal to' and so the dot on the end of the ray is left open. This means that 3 is not included in the solution.

SOLVING LINEAR INEQUATIONS

Linear inequations are solved in exactly the same way as are linear equations except when *dividing* or *multiplying* by a negative number. In these cases the sign changes to the opposite. Thus $\leq$ and $<$ change to $\geq$ and $>$ and vice versa.

The solution for inequalities is usually drawn on a number line.

Example

Solve the inequality $2x - 5 < 7$.

Solution

$$2x - 5 < 7$$
$$2x - 5 + 5 < 7 + 5 \qquad \text{Do the inverse operation of } - \text{ first, in the same way as for an equality.}$$
$$2x < 12 \qquad \text{Simplify. Here } -5 + 5 = 0 \text{ and } 7 + 5 = 12.$$
$$\frac{2x}{2} < \frac{12}{2} \qquad \text{Do the inverse operation of } \times \text{ next. Since the division is by a positive there is no need to change the } < \text{ sign.}$$
$$x < 6$$

Draw the result on the number line.

Example

Solve the inequality $\frac{r}{-5} + 1 \geq 2$.

Solution

$$\frac{r}{-5} + 1 \geq 2$$

$$\frac{r}{-5} + 1 - 1 \geq 2 - 1 \qquad \text{Do the inverse operation of } + \text{ first in the same way as for an equality.}$$

$$\frac{r}{-5} \geq 1$$

$$\frac{r}{-5} \times -5 \leq 1 \times -5 \qquad \text{The opposite of dividing by } -5 \text{ is to multiply by } -5. \text{ Since we are multiplying by a negative, the } \geq \text{ sign changes to the opposite } \leq.$$

$$r \leq -5$$

Draw the result on the number line.

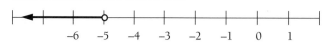

Example

Solve the inequality $8 - 4p > -12$.

Solution

$8 - 4p > -12$ When there is a negative in front of the variable, rewrite the equation with the negative term first.

$-4p + 8 > -12$

$-4p + 8 - 8 > -12 - 8$ *Take 8 from both sides as for an equality.*

$-4p > -20$

$\dfrac{-4p}{-4} < \dfrac{-20}{4}$ *Division by -4 is involved so change the $>$ sign to $<$.*

$p < 5$

Draw the result on the number line.

9 Indices and surds

You should know these power facts off by heart.

	Squares	Cubes	Fourth power	Fifth power
1	$1^2 = 1$	$1^3 = 1$	$1^4 = 1$	$1^5 = 1$
2	$2^2 = 4$	$2^3 = 8$	$2^4 = 16$	$2^5 = 32$
3	$3^2 = 9$	$3^3 = 27$	$3^4 = 81$	
4	$4^2 = 16$	$4^3 = 64$	$4^4 = 256$	
5	$5^2 = 25$	$5^3 = 125$	$5^4 = 625$	
6	$6^2 = 36$	$6^3 = 216$		
7	$7^2 = 49$			
8	$8^2 = 64$			
9	$9^2 = 81$			
10	$10^2 = 100$			
11	$11^2 = 121$			
12	$12^2 = 144$			
13	$13^2 = 169$			
14	$14^2 = 196$			
15	$15^2 = 225$			

INDICES

Indice Laws

Rule 1

$$a^m \times a^n = a^{m+n} \qquad \text{Powers multiplied} \rightarrow \text{indices added.}$$

Example

Simplify the following:
(a) $a^3 \times a^4$
(b) $2a^3 \times 3a^4$
(c) $d^5 + d^7$
(d) $3b^{10} - 5b^{10}$

Solution

(a) $a^3 \times a^4$
$= a^{3+4}$
$= a^7$

(b) $2a^3 \times 3a^4$ *Multiply the coefficients $2 \times 3 = 6$ first.*
$= 6a^{3+4}$
$= 6a^7$

(c) $d^5 + d^7$ is already fully simplified. It is not possible to simplify further as the powers are added and they are not like terms.

(d) $3b^{10} - 5b^{10}$ *These terms can be subtracted because they are like terms. They have the same*
$= -2b^{10}$ *base, b and the same index, 10.*

Rule 2

$$\frac{a^m}{a^n} = a^{m-n} \text{ or } (a^m \div a^n = a^{m-n}) \qquad \text{Powers divided} \rightarrow \text{indices subtracted.}$$

Example

Simplify the following:

(a) $\dfrac{a^7}{a^5}$ (b) $8k^{10} \div 2k^7$

Solution

(a) $\dfrac{a^7}{a^5} = a^2$

(b) $8k^{10} \div 2k^7 = 4k^3$ *Divide the constants first.*

Rule 3

$a^0 = 1$ *Anything to a zero index equals 1.*

Example

Simplify the following:
(a) $(28a)^0$ (b) $a^2 \times a \div a^3$

Solution

(a) $(28a)^0 = 1$
(b) $a^2 \times a \div a^3$
$= a^2 \times a^1 \div a^3$ *Add the indices of powers **multiplied** with the same base.*
$= a^{2+1-3}$ *Subtract the indices of powers **divided** with the same base.*
$= a^0$
$= 1$

Rule 4

$(a^m)^n = a^{mn}$ *When a power is raised to a power, multiply the indices.*

Example

Simplify $(b^5)^2$.

Solution
$(b^5)^2$
$= b^{10}$

Rule 5

$(ab)^n = a^n b^n$

Example

Simplify $\dfrac{(ab)^3}{ab^2}$

Solution

$\dfrac{(ab)^3}{ab^2}$

$= \dfrac{a^3 b^3}{ab^2}$ *Both a and b are raised to the power of 3.*

Rule 6

$\left(\dfrac{a}{b}\right)^n = \dfrac{a^n}{b^n}$

Mathematics Dictionary   Indices and surds

Example

Simplify $\left(\dfrac{b^3}{a}\right)^4$.

Solution

$$\left(\dfrac{b^3}{a}\right)^4$$

$$= \dfrac{(b^3)^4}{a^4}$$

$$= \dfrac{b^{12}}{a^4}$$

Rule 7

$a^{-n} = \dfrac{1}{a^n}$ and $a^n = \dfrac{1}{a^{-n}}$ To eliminate a negative, put the term on the other side of the vinculum. If a term to a negative power is in the numerator, put its positive version in the denominator. If it is in the denominator, put its positive version in the numerator.

Example

Simplify the following:
(a) $16a^7 \times 8a^{-3}$ (b) $\left(\dfrac{ab^{-1}}{b}\right)^2$ (c) $(ab)^{-3} \times a^2b^7$

Solution

(a) $16a^7 \times 8a^{-3}$

$$= \dfrac{16a^7 \times 8}{a^3} \quad \text{Deal with \textbf{negative} indices \textbf{first}.}$$

$$= 128a^{7-3}$$

$$= 128a^4$$

(b) $\left(\dfrac{ab^{-1}}{b}\right)^2$

$$= \left(\dfrac{a}{bb}\right)^2 \quad \text{Only the } b \text{ goes to the denominator since it alone is raised to the } -1.$$

$$= \dfrac{a^2}{(b^2)^2}$$

$$= \dfrac{a^2}{b^4}$$

(c) $(ab)^{-3} \times a^2b^7$

$$= \dfrac{a^2b^7}{(ab)^3} \quad \text{Because } (ab) \text{ is in brackets, all of the term } (ab) \text{ goes to the denominator when the negative is eliminated.}$$

$$= \dfrac{a^2b^7}{a^3b^3} \quad \text{Deal with each letter separately—all the } a\text{'s then all the } b\text{'s.}$$

$$= a^{2-3}b^{7-3}$$

$$= a^{-1}b^4$$

$$= \dfrac{b^4}{a}$$

Rule 8

$$a^{\frac{1}{2}} = \sqrt{a} \quad \text{and} \quad a^{\frac{p}{q}} = (\sqrt[q]{a})^p$$

Example

Simplify the following:
(a) $16^{\frac{3}{4}}$
(b) $(16a^8b^4)^{\frac{3}{4}}$

Solution

(a) $16^{\frac{3}{4}}$
$= [(16)^{\frac{1}{4}}]^3$
$= 2^3$
$= 8$

Calculator steps: 16 $\boxed{y^x}$ (3 $\boxed{a^b/c}$ 4)

(b) $(16a^8b^4)^{\frac{3}{4}}$ *Deal with $\frac{3}{4}$ first.*
$= (16^{\frac{3}{4}})(a^8)^{\frac{3}{4}}(b^4)^{\frac{3}{4}}$ *Work from outside in.*
$= 2^3 a^{(8 \times \frac{3}{4})} b^{(4 \times \frac{3}{4})}$
$= 8a^6b^3$

Notes

- $\sqrt[4]{16} = 2$ and $2^4 = 16$ and $16^{\frac{1}{4}} = 2$ give the same information.

- $8^{-2} = \dfrac{1}{8^2} = \dfrac{1}{64}$ and $625^{\frac{-1}{4}} = \dfrac{1}{625^{\frac{1}{4}}} = \dfrac{1}{5}$

When dealing with fractional indices on the calculator, use *brackets around the fraction*.

Example:

$(1\frac{2}{3})^{(\frac{3}{4})}$

Calculator steps: 1 $\boxed{a^b/c}$ 2 $\boxed{a^b/c}$ 3 $\boxed{y^x}$ (3 $\boxed{a^b/c}$ 4) $\boxed{=}$

SURDS

Irrational roots, such as $\sqrt{2}$ and $\sqrt{7}$, are known as surds.

Surdic rules

$\sqrt{a} \times \sqrt{a} = a$

$\sqrt{ab} = \sqrt{a} \times \sqrt{b}$

$\sqrt{\dfrac{a}{b}} = \dfrac{\sqrt{a}}{\sqrt{b}}$

$\sqrt{a}(\sqrt{b} - \sqrt{c}) = \sqrt{a}\sqrt{b} - \sqrt{a}\sqrt{c}$

Example

Simplify the following:
(a) $\sqrt{5} \times \sqrt{15}$
(b) $\sqrt{12}$
(c) $\dfrac{\sqrt{72}}{\sqrt{2}}$
(d) $\sqrt{5}(\sqrt{15} - \sqrt{2})$

Solution

(a) $\sqrt{5} \times \sqrt{15}$
$= \sqrt{5} \times \sqrt{5 \times 3}$
$= 5\sqrt{3}$

(b) $\sqrt{12}$ Look for factors of 12 that are perfect squares, like 4.
$= \sqrt{4} \times \sqrt{3}$
$= 2\sqrt{3}$

(c) $\dfrac{\sqrt{72}}{\sqrt{2}}$
$= \sqrt{\dfrac{72}{2}}$
$= \sqrt{36}$
$= 6$

(d) $\sqrt{5}(\sqrt{15} - \sqrt{2})$
$= \sqrt{5} \times \sqrt{15} - \sqrt{5} \times \sqrt{2}$
$= \sqrt{5} \times \sqrt{5} \times \sqrt{3} - \sqrt{10}$
$= 5\sqrt{3} - \sqrt{10}$

Rationalising a denominator

If the denominator is a *single term*, multiply the numerator and denominator by the surdic part of the denominator.

Example

Rationalise the denominator in the following:

(a) $\dfrac{2}{\sqrt{3}}$ (b) $\dfrac{3}{4\sqrt{7}}$

Solution

(a) $\dfrac{2}{\sqrt{3}}$
$= \dfrac{2 \times \sqrt{3}}{\sqrt{3} \times \sqrt{3}}$
$= \dfrac{2\sqrt{3}}{3}$

(b) $\dfrac{3}{4\sqrt{7}}$
$= \dfrac{3 \times \sqrt{7}}{4\sqrt{7} \times \sqrt{7}}$ Multiply by the surd part of the denominator only.
$= \dfrac{3\sqrt{7}}{28}$

If the denominator has *two terms*, multiply the numerator and denominator by the **binomial conjugate**. The conjugate of $a + b$ is $a - b$, that is the second term changes sign.

Example

Rationalise the denominator in the following:

(a) $\dfrac{2 + \sqrt{3}}{1 - \sqrt{5}}$ (b) $\dfrac{5}{\sqrt{7} + \sqrt{3}}$

Solution

(a) $\dfrac{2 + \sqrt{3}}{1 - \sqrt{5}}$
$= \dfrac{(2 + \sqrt{3})}{(1 - \sqrt{5})} \times \dfrac{(1 + \sqrt{5})}{(1 + \sqrt{5})}$ A vinculum implies brackets.
$= \dfrac{(2 + \sqrt{3})(1 + \sqrt{5})}{1 - 5}$ Difference between two squares: $(1 - \sqrt{5})(1 + \sqrt{5}) = 1 - 5$.
$= \dfrac{2 + \sqrt{3} + 2\sqrt{5} + \sqrt{15}}{-4}$

(b) $\dfrac{5}{\sqrt{7}+\sqrt{3}}$

$= \dfrac{5}{(\sqrt{7}+\sqrt{3})} \times \dfrac{(\sqrt{7}-\sqrt{3})}{(\sqrt{7}-\sqrt{3})}$

$= \dfrac{5\sqrt{7}-5\sqrt{3}}{7-3}$

$= \dfrac{5\sqrt{7}-5\sqrt{3}}{4}$

STANDARD FORM (SCIENTIFIC NOTATION)

A number in **standard form** or **scientific notation** takes the form of a number between 1 and 10 multiplied by a power of 10.

Example

Write the following numbers in standard form:
(a) 204 000
(b) 0.000 65

Solution
(a) $204\,000 = 2.04 \times 10^5$ 2.04 is between 1 and 10. Shift the number 5 places to the right of the decimal point.
(b) $0.000\,65 = 6.5 \times 10^{-4}$ 6.5 is between 1 and 10. Shift the number 4 places to the left of the decimal point. Use a **negative** index to show the number has become smaller.

Example

Write the following numbers as an ordinary number:
(a) 3.57×10^3
(b) 5.087×10^{-6}

Solution
(a) 3.57×10^3
$= 3.57 \times 1000$ Shift the number 3 places to the right of the decimal point.
$= 3570$
(b) 5.087×10^{-6}
$= 5.087 \div 1\,000\,000$ The division occurs because 10^{-6} means to divide by 10^6. Shift the decimal number 6 places to the left of the decimal point.
$= 0.000\,005\,087$

- The standard form of a *small number* will involve a **negative** index.
- The standard form of a *large number* will involve a **positive** index.

Scientific notation on the calculator

The calculator uses scientific notation to display large and small numbers.

Example

Write the ordinary number for a calculator display which says:
(a) 1.69×10^4
(b) 1.09×10^{-5}

Solution
(a) $1.69 \times 10^4 = 1.69 \times 10\,000$
$= 16\,900$ The number moves 4 places to the left of the decimal point.
(b) $1.09 \times 10^{-5} = 1.09 \div 100\,000$
$= 0.000\,010\,9$ The number moves 5 places to the right of the decimal point.

10 Ratio, rate, proportion and scale

RATIO

Ratio is used to compare *two quantities of the same kind*. The order of the quantities is important.
A ratio is written as *a* : *b*. Units are not included. The colon ':' is stated as 'is to'. Thus *a* : *b* means *a* is to *b*.

Example

In this diagram, find the ratio of the:
(a) shaded area to unshaded area
(b) unshaded area to shaded area
(c) unshaded area to total area

Solution
(a) shaded : unshaded = 1 : 3
(b) unshaded : shaded = 3 : 1
(c) unshaded : total = 3 : 4

Simplifying ratios

Ratios are dealt with most easily when they are in **simplest form**.
For example, the ratio of the shaded area : unshaded area = 4 : 16.
This can also be expressed as the ratio 1 : 4   *Dividing both by 4.*
The ratio 1 : 4 is said to be in simplest form.
The following examples show various ways to simplify ratios.

Example

Simplify 45 : 100.

Solution
   45 : 100   *Divide both values by 5.*
= 9 : 20

Example

Simplify 2.8 : 0.56.

Solution
   2.8 : 0.56   *Multiply both numbers by the greatest number of decimal places. Here it is 2 decimal places in the number 0.56.*
= 280 : 56
= 35 : 7   *Divide by 8.*
= 5 : 1   *Divide by 7.*

Example

Simplify 3 m : 400 cm.

Solution
   3m : 400 cm
= 300 cm : 400 cm   *Convert the bigger unit to the smaller unit.*
= 3 : 4   *Divide both sides by 100.*

When simplifying ratios that involve fractions, we use the rule of **cross-multiplication**. This rule states that:
$$\frac{a}{b} : \frac{c}{d} = a \times d : c \times b.$$
The values are multiplied in a cross direction. Always *start* with the *first top value*.

Example

Simplify $\frac{8}{15} : \frac{4}{7}$.

Solution

$\frac{8}{15} : \frac{4}{7}$

$= 8 \times 7 : 4 \times 15$ *Cross-multiply starting with the first top value.*

$= 56 : 60$ *Evaluate and then divide both sides by 4.*

$= 14 : 15$

Example

Simplify $2\frac{2}{3} : 4\frac{1}{5}$.

Solution

$2\frac{2}{3} : 4\frac{1}{5}$ *Change to improper fractions first.*

$= \frac{8}{3} : \frac{21}{5}$ *Cross-multiply.*

$= 40 : 63$ *Can't simplify further.*

Finding equivalent ratios

If the ratios $a : b$ and $c : d$ are equivalent, then $\frac{a}{b} = \frac{c}{d}$ and $a \times d = b \times c$, again using cross-multiplication.

Example

Show that $3 : 2 = 6 : 4$.

Solution

The ratios are equivalent if $\frac{3}{2} = \frac{6}{4}$ and $3 \times 4 = 2 \times 6$.

This is true, and so the ratios are equal.

Example

Find x if $5 : 2 = x : 4$.

Solution

If the ratios are equivalent

$\frac{5}{2} = \frac{x}{4}$

$5 \times 4 = 2 \times x$

$20 = 2x$

$\frac{20}{2} = \frac{2x}{2}$

$10 = x$

Division of a quantity according to a given ratio

One of the most common uses for ratio is when dividing a quantity equally between two or more parties.

Example

Divide $200 between Tehani and Sing in the ratio of 7 : 3.

Solution
1. Add each part of the ratio to get the total number of parts: $7 + 3 = 10$
2. Divide this number into the total to get the value of each part: $\frac{200}{10} = 20$
3. Tehani : Sing
   7 : 3
   $7 \times 20 : 3 \times 20$
   $140 : $60   Tehani gets $140 and Sing gets $60.

Example

A fertiliser is made up of emulsion, phosphorus and water in the ratio of 3 : 1 : 4. If a quantity of 1600 litres is to be made, how many litres of emulsion will be needed?

Solution
1. Add each part of the ratio to get the total number of parts: $3 + 1 + 4 = 8$
2. Divide this number into the total to get the value of each part: $\frac{1600}{8} = 200$
3. emulsion : phosphorus : water
   3 : 1 : 4
   $3 \times 200 : 1 \times 200 : 4 \times 200$
   600 : 200 : 800   Hence, 600 litres of emulsion is needed.

RATE

A **rate** compares *quantities of a different kind* in an ordered way. Units are included when writing a rate. Some examples of rates are: kilometres per hour; words per minute; litres per minute; and dollars per hour. The use of the symbol '/', which means 'per', is used to write rates concisely, as in km/h, words/min, L/min and $/h.
Rate is commonly used to compare distance and time and is called speed:

$$\frac{\text{Distance}}{\text{Time}} = \text{Speed}$$

Example

Express 18 km in 2 hours as a single unit.

Solution

$\frac{18 \text{ km}}{2 \text{ h}} = 9$ km/h

Example

Convert 25 km/h to m/s.

Solution

$\frac{25 \text{ km}}{1 \text{ h}}$

$= \frac{25 \times 1000 \text{ m}}{60 \times 60 \text{ s}}$ There are 60×60 s in 1 h.

$= 6.94$ m/s

Example

Convert 40 m/s to km/h.

Solution

$$\frac{40 \text{ m}}{1 \text{ s}}$$

$$= \frac{(40 \div 1000) \text{ km}}{[1 \div (60 \times 60)] \text{ s}} \quad \textit{These brackets must be used when entering the quotient into the calculator.}$$

$$= 144 \text{ km/h}$$

Rate comparisons

Rates are also used for price comparisons.

Example

Washing powder is available in a 10 kg bucket for $41.50. It is also available in 2.5 kg packets for $10.70. Which is the better value for money and by how much?

Solution

The bucket: 10 kg for $41.50
  1 kg costs $41.50 ÷ 10 = $4.15
The packet: 2.5 kg for $10.70
  1 kg costs $10.70 ÷ 2.5 = $4.28
Hence, the bulk buy in the bucket is better value by ($4.28 − $4.15) = 13c/kg.

SCALE

A **scale drawing** is either *smaller* or *larger* than the original object but its dimensions are in the same proportion. Hence, the **ratios** of corresponding measures are the *same*.

The scale drawing of an object has all its measurements in the same ratio as the original.

A **scale factor** is used to *multiply* all the measurements of one object to get the measurements of the new object. Scale information is generally written as a ratio, as in $a : b$.

- When a is the *larger value*, as in 4 : 1, the scaled object will be *enlarged*, that is, larger than the original.

In this diagram, which shows two scaled objects, the circle measurements double and the rectangle measurements double.

 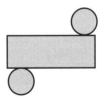

- When a is the *smaller value*, as in 1 : 2, the scaled object will be *reduced* in size, that is, smaller than the original.

Any measurement in the second diagram is half that of the first. Hence, the scale factor $= \frac{1}{2}$ or 0.5.

PROPORTION

Many quantities are in either *direct* or *indirect* **proportion**. This means that a change in one quantity causes a *proportional* change in another.

Direct proportion

Two quantities are in **direct proportion** if an *increase* in one causes an *increase* in the other. Some examples include:
- the speed of travel and the distance travelled in a certain time
- the number of people at a party and the food required to feed them

A *graph* of direct proportion will look like this:

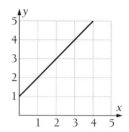

Indirect or inverse proportion

Two quantities are in **inverse** (or **indirect**) **proportion** if an *increase* in one causes a *decrease* in the other. Some examples include:
- the number of people working and the time taken to do the job
- the speed of travel and the time taken to complete the journey

A *graph* of indirect proportion will look like this:

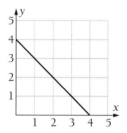

Neither direct nor inverse proportion.

Some quantities are in *neither direct* nor *inverse proportion*. Some examples include:
- the number of people running a race and the time it takes to run the race
- the height of a human and their age

Problem solving with proportion

If two things are in *direct* proportion, their ratios are equal:

$$a : b = c : d \Leftrightarrow \frac{a}{b} = \frac{c}{d}$$

Example

500 mL of juice costs $1.50. How much is a 1.5 L bottle?

Solution

1. Set the question out under headings.

Quantity of juice	Cost
500 mL	$1.50
1.5 L = 1500 mL	x

Use the same unit for each ratio, so 1.5 L = 1500 mL.

2. Decide if the question is direct or indirect.
   More juice means *more* money. Hence, this question is direct. The ratios, found under the headings above, are equal.

$$\frac{500}{1500} = \frac{1.5}{x}$$

$500 \times x = 1.5 \times 1500$ *Cross-multiply.*

$$x = \frac{1.5 \times 1500}{500}$$

$x = \$4.50$

If two things are in *inverse* proportion, their inverse ratios are *equal*:

$$a : b = c : d \Leftrightarrow \frac{a}{b} = \frac{d}{c}$$

Example

Four men can finish building a house in 8 weeks. How long will it take 5 men?

Solution

1. Set the question out under headings.

Number of men	Number of days
4	8
5	x

2. Decide if the question is direct or indirect.
   More men means *less* time building. Hence, this question involves inverse proportion. Invert one of the ratios.

   $$\frac{4}{5} = \frac{x}{8}$$

   $4 \times 8 = 5 \times x$ *Cross-multiply.*
   $32 = 5x$
   $\frac{32}{5} = x$
   $6.4 \text{ weeks} = x$

A feature of indirect proportion is that it describes situations in which the *product of two variables remains constant*.

11 Functions

THE CARTESIAN PLANE

The **cartesian plane** is a system for locating points using horizontal and vertical directions. We are familiar with giving directions as north, south, east and west. The cartesian plane is a similar system.
- the x-axis is horizontal and the y-axis is vertical
- there are positive and negative values on both axes
- the origin is the point $(0, 0)$

The following diagrams of the cartesian plane give information about each one of its four parts.
- In the 1st quadrant, move in a positive direction forward and a positive direction up.

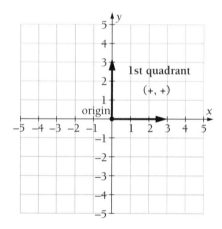

- In the 2nd quadrant, move in a negative direction backward and a positive direction up.

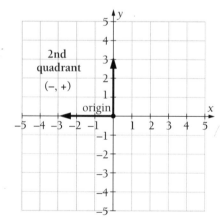

- In the 3rd quadrant, move in a negative direction backward and a negative direction down.

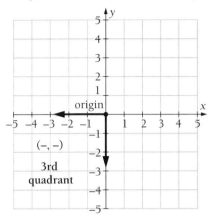

- In the 4th quadrant, move in a positive direction forward and a negative direction down.

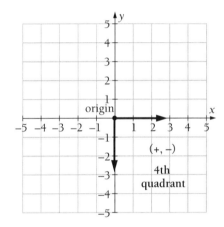

ORDERED PAIRS AND PLOTTING POINTS

Every point on the cartesian plane is defined by an ordered pair, which is written as: (x-coordinate, y-coordinate). The x-coordinate is in the *first* place and the y-coordinate in the *second* place.

The x-coordinate tells the distance from the origin in a *horizontal* direction. If the direction is *right*, the value is *positive*; if the direction is *left* the value is *negative*.

The y-coordinate tells the distance from the origin in a *vertical* direction. If the direction is *up*, the value is *positive*; if the direction is *down*, the value is *negative*.

Example

Some ordered pairs are graphed on the cartesian plane on page 72.
(a) Give the coordinates of the ordered pairs A, B, C, D.
(b) Mark the ordered pairs (3, 4) (–1, 0) (3, –5) (–4, –5) (0, 0) and (0, 1) on the plane.

Solution
(a) The ordered pair at A = (2, 3)   2 to the right along the x-axis, 3 up the y-axis.
    The ordered pair at B = (–3, –2)   3 to the left along the x-axis, 2 down the y-axis.
    The ordered pair at C = (–4, 4)   4 to the left along the x-axis, 4 up the y-axis.
    The ordered pair at D = (0, –3)   0 along the x-axis, 3 down the y-axis.
(b) When looking at these solutions, think about why you think this cartesian plane system is sometimes called the rectangular coordinate system.

- For (3, 4), move 3 units in a positive direction on the x-axis, and 4 units in a positive direction on the y-axis.
- For (–1, 0) move 1 unit in a negative direction on the x-axis, and 0 units on the y-axis.
- For (3, –5) move 3 units in a positive direction on the x-axis, and 5 units in a negative direction on the y-axis.
- For (–4, –5) move 4 units in a negative direction on the x-axis, and 5 units in a negative direction on the y-axis.
- For (0, 0) move 0 units on the x-axis, and 0 units on the y-axis.
- For (0, 1) move 0 units on the x-axis, and 1 unit in a positive direction on the y-axis.

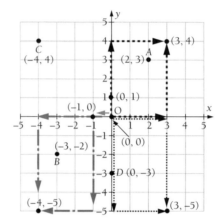

LINEAR FUNCTIONS

A **function** is a set of ordered pairs where *every x value* has a *unique y value*. The rules $y = x + 1$ and $y = 2x - 1$ are examples of *functions*—for every x value there is a unique y value.

Rules that are functions are written using the terminology $f(x)$, which means the function at the value of x: x is called the **input** and $f(x)$ is called the **output**.

Hence, the rule $y = x + 1$ can be written as $f(x) = x + 1$, and the rule $y = 2x - 1$ can be written as $f(x) = 2x - 1$.

Example

For the function $f(x) = x + 1$:
(a) state the meaning of $f(1)$ (b) find the value of the function at $x = 1$
(c) find the value of x at $f(x) = 17$

Solution
(a) $f(1)$ means the value of $f(x) = x + 1$ at $x = 1$
(b) $f(x) = x + 1$
$f(1) = 1 + 1$
$= 2$
(c) $f(x) = 17$
$17 = x + 1$
$16 = x$

Ordered pairs that are part of a function have a clear pattern. On this graph, those marked with a • form a straight line. When these ordered pairs are written in a **table of values**, a pattern emerges:

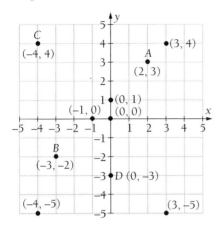

x	-3	-1	0	2	3
y	-2	0	1	3	4

x	-3	-1	0	2	3
x + 1	-3 + 1	-1 + 1	0 + 1	2 + 1	3 + 1
y	-2	0	1	3	4

It is clear that y and $x + 1$ are the same. Hence, for this set of ordered pairs the rule linking x and $y + 1$ is said to be a **linear function**.

Example

(a) Complete this table of values for the linear function $y = 2x - 1$:

x	-1	0	2	3
y				

(b) List the ordered pairs from the table.
(c) Plot these ordered pairs on a cartesian plane and draw the linear function.

Solution

(a) To find the values of y for the x values given, substitute the x value into the rule $y = 2x - 1$.
When $x = -1$, $y = 2x - 1 = 2 \times -1 - 1 = -2 - 1 = -3$. Hence, this ordered pair is $(-1, -3)$.
The other ordered pairs can be found in a similar manner to give the table of values:

x	-1	0	2	3
y	-3	-1	3	5

(b) The ordered pairs from this table are {(-1, -3), (0, -1), (2, 3), (3, 5)}.

(c) A graph of this linear function is:

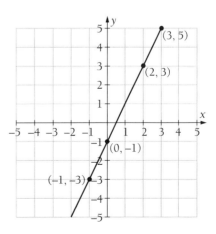

Mathematics Dictionary Functions

ALGEBRAIC FORMAT FOR LINEAR FUNCTIONS

A linear function takes the form $f(x) = mx + c$ or $y = mx + c$ where m and c are constants. The exponent of x for a linear function is 1.

- $y = -3x + 5$ is a linear function where $m = -3$ and $c = 5$.
- $f(x) = 2x$ is a linear function where $m = 2$ and $c = 0$.
- $f(x) = x^2 + 1$ is not a linear function since the exponent of x is 2.

Example

Determine if the following patterns are linear and, if so, name the m and c values.
(a) $f(x) = 2x + 7$
(b) $t = -3p - 4$
(c) $z = 4x^2 + 3x$

Solution
(a) and (b) are linear, (c) is not.
For (a), $m = 2$ and $c = 7$
For (b), $m = -3$ and $c = -4$

Example

Rearrange the following equations to the form $y = mx + c$ and name the m and c values:
(a) $4x + y = 1$
(b) $3x + 2y = 6$

Solution
(a) $4x + y = 1$
       $y = -4x + 1$
       $m = -4$ and $c = 1$
(b)   We need to isolate y therefore:
       $3x + 2y = 6$
       $2y = -3x + 6$
       $y = -\frac{3}{2}x + 3$
       $m = -\frac{3}{2}$ and $c = 3$

LINKING ORDERED PAIRS AND LINEAR GRAPHS

If an ordered pair satisfies a linear function (fits the pattern), it will lie on its line. If an ordered pair does not satisfy the linear function, it will not lie on its line.

This graph shows the function $f(x) = x - 1$.
By drawing a vertical line from 2 on the x-axis to the line, and a horizontal line across to 1 on the y-axis, it can be seen that when $x = 2$, $y = 1$ (see arrows).

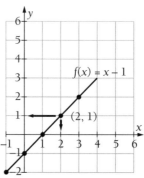

Example

(a) Using a similar method, extend this table of values.

x	−1	0	1	2	3	4
y			1			

(b) (2, 2) is an ordered pair that does not fit this pattern or the line. Name another and mark it on your graph.

(c) Show by substitution that (2, 2) does not fit the function $f(x) = x - 1$.

Solution

(a) The table of values is:

x	−1	0	1	2	3	4
y	−2	−1	0	1	2	3

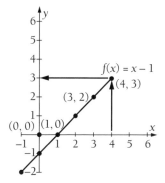

(b) Any ordered pair that is not on the line will do. Here the point chosen is the origin (0, 0).

(c) $y = x - 1$
$2 = 2 - 1$. This is false.
Hence, (2, 2) does not lie on the line $y = x - 1$.

DOMAIN AND RANGE

When given information in function form, the variables are named according to their role. The variable that contains the input data is called the **independent variable**. It is in the first position of an ordered pair or the first row in a table of values. The variable that contains the output data is called the **dependent variable**. It is in the second position of an ordered pair or the second row in a table of values. The dependent variable is so named because it changes value depending on the value of the independent variable.

Example

This is the graph of the function $y = \sqrt{x}$.
Name its domain and range.

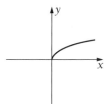

Solution

Domain: $x \geq 0$, $x \in R$ *R is the set of real numbers.*
Range: $y \geq 0$, $y \in R$.

Example

For the function {(0, 1), (1, 2), (2, 3), (3, 4)}, name its domain and range.

Solution

Domain: {0, 1, 2, 3}
Range: {1, 2, 3, 4}

GRADIENT (SLOPE)

Linear functions graphed as *straight lines* have a *constant* **gradient**. The **slope** is the same at any point on the line.

Gradient or slope is defined as: $\frac{\text{change in } y}{\text{change in } x}$. This can also be written as $\frac{\Delta y}{\Delta x}$.

Sometimes this is defined as $\frac{\text{rise}}{\text{run}}$ or $\frac{\text{vertical change}}{\text{horizontal change}}$.

Finding gradient using formulae

The line opposite joins the points $A(x_A, y_A)$ and $B(x_B, y_B)$.
   The change in y (vertical change) is shown by the dashed bracket and equals $y_B - y_A$
   The change in x (horizontal change) is shown by the solid bracket and equals $x_B - x_A$.

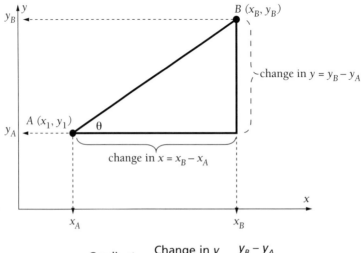

$$\text{Gradient} = \frac{\text{Change in } y}{\text{Change in } x} = \frac{y_B - y_A}{x_B - x_A}$$

Gradient = $\tan \theta°$, where $\theta°$ is the angle made with the positive direction of the *x*-axis, as shown.

Lines that slope in a *forward* direction have a *positive* gradient and are sometimes called *rising* lines. The line $y = 2x - 1$ has a positive gradient of 2.

This line is rising.

Lines that slope in a *backwards* direction and have a *negative* gradient are sometimes called *falling* lines. The line $y = -\frac{1}{3}x - 7$ has a negative gradient of $\frac{-1}{3}$.

These lines are falling.

Example

Find the gradient of the line joining A and B.

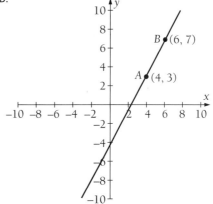

Solution

Hence, $x_A = 4$, $y_A = 3$, $x_B = 6$, $y_B = 7$

$$\text{Gradient} = \frac{y_B - y_A}{x_B - x_A}$$

$$= \frac{7 - 3}{6 - 4}$$

$$= \frac{4}{2}$$

$$= 2$$

Example

Find the gradient of the line joining (–1, 6) and (–3, 5).

Solution

$$\text{Gradient} = \frac{y_B - y_A}{x_B - x_A}$$

$$= \frac{5 - 6}{-3 - 1}$$

$$= \frac{-1}{-3 + 1}$$

$$= \frac{-1}{-2}$$

$$= \frac{1}{2}$$

Example

Is the line joining (1, 1) and (3, –1) rising or falling?

Solution

If the gradient is negative, the line is falling. If the gradient is positive, the line is rising.

$$\text{Gradient} = \frac{y_B - y_A}{x_B - x_A}$$

$$= \frac{-1 - 1}{3 - 1}$$

$$= \frac{-2}{2}$$

$$= -1 \quad \text{The gradient is negative so the line is falling.}$$

Practical applications of slope

The steepness of line graphs can be interpreted as a rate of change. Line graphs can be used to determine three very common rates:

- Speed $= \dfrac{\text{Change in distance}}{\text{Change in time}}$

- Acceleration $= \dfrac{\text{Change in speed}}{\text{Change in time}}$

- Flow rate $= \dfrac{\text{Change in volume}}{\text{Change in time}}$

FORMS OF LINEAR EQUATIONS

- The **x-intercept** is where a curve cuts the x-axis and takes the form $(a, 0)$.
- The **y-intercept** is where a curve cuts the y-axis and takes the form $(0, a)$.

Gradient and y-intercept form

When given a gradient m and y-intercept c, the equation of the line is $y = mx + c$.

Example

Find the equation of the line through $(0, 9)$ with a gradient of 5.

Solution

Equation is: $y = mx + c$
$y = 5x + 9$

Gradient and one point form

When given a gradient m and one point (x_1, y_1), the equation of the line is $y - y_1 = m(x - x_1)$.

Example

Find the equation of the line through $(1, 9)$ with a gradient of -2.

Solution

Equation is:
$y - y_1 = m(x - x_1)$
$y - 9 = -2(x - 1)$
$y - 9 = -2x + 2$
$y = -2x + 11$

General form

The **general form** of a straight line is $ax + by + c = 0$.

Example

Rearrange the line $y = 6x - 3$ into general form.

Solution

$y = 6x - 3$
General form is: $6x - y - 3 = 0$

Two point form

When given two points (x_1, y_1) and (x_2, y_2) the equation of the line joining them is $y - y_1 = \dfrac{y_2 - y_1}{x_2 - x_1}(x - x_1)$

Example

Find the equation of the line through $(4, 5)$ and $(2, -3)$.

Solution

$y - 5 = \dfrac{y_2 - y_1}{x_2 - x_1}$

$y - 5 = \left(\dfrac{-3 - 5}{2 - 4}\right)(x - 4)$

$y - 5 = 4(x - 4)$
$y - 5 = 4x - 16$
$y = 4x - 11$

Parallel to the x-axis

A line parallel to the x-axis takes the form: $y = c$. The equation to the x-axis is: $y = 0$.

Example

Find the equation of the line parallel to the x-axis and through the point (0, –1).

Solution
Equation is: $y = -1$

Parallel to the y-axis

A line parallel to the y-axis takes the form $x = a$. The equation to the y-axis is $x = 0$.

Example

Find the equation of the line parallel to the y-axis, through the point (5, 0).

Solution
Equation is: $x = 5$

METHODS OF SKETCHING A STRAIGHT LINE
Using the graphics calculator Casio 9850

Example

Graph the function $y = 3x - 5$ using the graphics calculator.

Solution
1. Clearing the calculator:

    (a) If you make a mistake at any stage press [QUIT] and start again.

    (b) If the calculator 'locks up' like a computer does, press [SHIFT] [ON].

    (c) Turn the calculator on and choose [MEM] with the arrow keys. Press [EXE].

    (d) Choose [RESET] [EXE] [F1] [YES].

2. Graph the function $y = 3x - 5$.

    (a) Press [MENU] [GRAPH] [EXE].

    (b) Next to Y1, press 3 [X, T] –5 [EXE]. (The calculator button for x is [X, T].)

    (c) Press [F6] [DRAW].

    (d) Press [SHIFT] [F1] to trace along the function. A trace shows the co-ordinates of each point in turn at the bottom of the screen. A little marker (+) appears on the screen. Use the left and right arrow keys to get the marker to move along. You may need to press it several times before you see it.

    (e) Press [EXIT].

The table of values method

Example

Use a table of values to draw the line $y = 3x - 4$ for $-3 \leq x \leq 2$.

Solution

Draw up a table of values including the first value for *x*, which is –3, and the last value for *x*, which is 2, and $x = 0$, as shown below.

x	-3	0	2
y			

Substitute the values for *x* into the equation in turn.

If $x = -3$, $y = 3 \times -3 - 4 = -13$, ∴ (–3, –13) lies on the line.
If $x = 0$, $y = 3 \times 0 - 4 = -4$, ∴ (0, –4) lies on the line.
If $x = 2$, $y = 3 \times 2 - 4 = 2$, ∴ (2, 2) lies on the line.

Complete the table of values:

x	-3	0	2
y	-13	-4	0

Plot the ordered pairs and draw the line. Name the line and name the axes.

The double intercept method

Example

Use the double intercept method to draw the line $2y = -5x + 1$.

Solution

Put $x = 0$:
$2y = -5x + 1$
$2y = -5 \times 0 + 1$
$2y = 1$
$y = \frac{1}{2}$ The *y*-intercept is $(0, \frac{1}{2}) = (0, 0.5)$.

Put $y = 0$:
$2y = -5x + 1$
$2 \times 0 = -5x + 1$
$1 = -5x + 1$
$-1 = -5x$
$\frac{-1}{-5} = x$ or $x = 0.2$ The *x*-intercept is $(\frac{1}{5}, 0) = (0.2, 0)$.

Plot the ordered pairs and draw the line. Name the line, points and axes.
This method of drawing a line is very useful because it gives the *x*- and *y*-intercepts. It does not work, however, for lines of the form $y = mx$, which pass through the origin. Use the table of values method for these lines.

The gradient and y-intercept method

Example

Use the gradient and y-intercept method to draw the following lines.

(a) $y = \frac{2}{3}x - 1$ (b) $y = 3x - 2$ (c) $y = -\frac{4}{5}x + 3$

Solution

The line must be put in the form of $y = mx + c$, where m is the gradient and c is the y-intercept. Even when the value of m is a fraction this method is easy and fast.

(a) $y = \frac{2}{3}x - 1$: m is positive
- Start at −1 on the y-axis.

- Go up for 2.

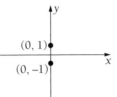

- Go right for 3 (a positive gradient).

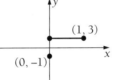

- Join the first and last points.

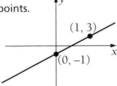

(b) $y = 3x - 2$ is the same as $y = \frac{3}{1}x - 2$
- Start at −2 on the y-axis.
- Go up for 3.
- Go right for 1.
- Join the first and last points.

(c) $y = -\frac{4}{5}x + 3$: m is negative.
- Start at 3 on the y-axis.
- Go up for 4.
- Go left for 5 (for a negative gradient)
- Join the first and last points.

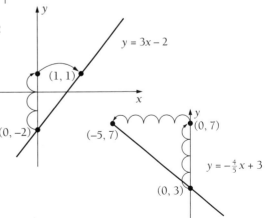

LINES PARALLEL TO THE AXES

Example

Find the equation to the line parallel to the *x*-axis and through the point (0, −1).

Solution

Note that every point on this line has a y-co-ordinate of −1

A horizontal line has a gradient of 0.
Hence, the equation is: $y = mx + c$
$y = 0 \times x + -1$
$y = -1$

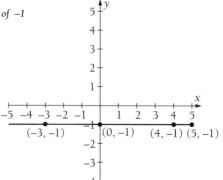

Example

Find the equation to the line parallel to the *y*-axis and through the point (5, 0).

Solution

Note that every point on this line has an x-co-ordinate of 5.

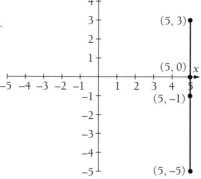

Example

Draw the line $x = 2$.

Solution

This line is parallel to the *y*-axis and passes through the point (2, 0).

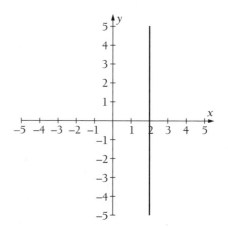

Example

Find the equation to the following line.

Solution

This line is parallel to the x-axis and passes through the point (0, −1). Hence, its equation is $y = -1$.

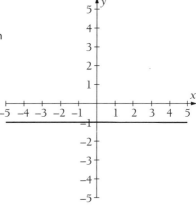

SPECIAL LINES AND THEIR GRADIENTS

- **Parallel lines** never meet. If m_1 and m_2 are the gradients of the two parallel lines, then $m_1 = m_2$. They have *equal* gradients. Hence, $y = 3x + 5$ is parallel to $y = 3x - 7$ since both have the gradient $m = 3$.
- **Perpendicular lines** are at right angles to each other. If m_1 and m_2 are the gradients of the two perpendicular lines, then $m_1 \times m_2 = -1$. Hence, $y = 3x + 5$ is perpendicular to $y = -\frac{1}{3}x - 7$ since their gradients are 3 and $-\frac{1}{3}$ and $3 \times -\frac{1}{3} = -1$.
- **Collinear points** lie on a straight line. A, B and C are collinear if the gradient of AB equals the gradient of BC, which equals the gradient of AC.

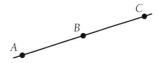

Example

Name any parallel or perpendicular lines from the following list:

$y = 3x + 1$ $y = \frac{1}{3}x + 3$ $y = 3x + 9$ $y = 2x - 6$ $y = -\frac{1}{2}x + 6$

Solution

The lines $y = 3x + 1$ and $y = 3x + 9$ are parallel since they both have a gradient of 3.
The lines $y = 2x - 6$ and $y = -\frac{1}{2}x + 6$ are perpendicular since their gradients multiply to give −1.

Example

Are the following points collinear? $A = (1, 4)$, $B = (2, 5)$ and $C = (-3, 0)$

Solution

$$\text{Gradient of } AB = \frac{y_B - y_A}{x_B - x_A}$$

$$= \frac{5 - 4}{2 - 1}$$

$$= 1$$

$$\text{Gradient of } BC = \frac{0 - 5}{-3 - 2}$$

$$= \frac{-5}{-5}$$

$$= 1$$

The gradients are equal and therefore the three points are collinear.

DISTANCE FORMULA

If $A = (x_1, y_1)$ and $B = (x_2, y_2)$,

$$m_{AB} = \sqrt{(x_2 - x_1)^2 + (y_2 - y_1)^2}.$$

Example

Find the distance between the two points (−4, 7) and (1, −2).

Solution

$$\begin{aligned} m_{AB} &= \sqrt{(1 - -4)^2 + (-2 - 7)^2} \\ &= \sqrt{106} \\ &= 10.3 \end{aligned}$$

MIDPOINT FORMULA

If $A = (x_1, y_1)$ and $B = (x_2, y_2)$; then M is the midpoint equidistant from A and B.

$$M = (x_m, y_m) = \left(\frac{x_1 + x_2}{2}, \frac{y_1 + y_2}{2}\right)$$

Example

Find the midpoint between the two points (−4, 7) and (1, −2).

Solution

$$\left(\frac{x_1 + x_2}{2}, \frac{y_1 + y_2}{2}\right) = \left(\frac{-4 + 1}{2}, \frac{7 - 2}{2}\right)$$

$$M = (-1.5, 2.5)$$

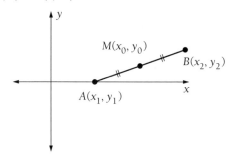

SIMULTANEOUS EQUATIONS

Solving a set of simultaneous equations means to find ordered pairs that lie on both equations. These ordered pairs will, in turn, satisfy both equations. The solution is where the graphs intersect.

Methods of solving simultaneous equations

Method 1: With the graphics calculator

Example

Solve the following simultaneous equations using the graphics calculator Casio 9850.
(a) $y = x$
(b) $y = 2x - 1$

Solution
- Draw the two functions $f(x) = x$ and $f(x) = 2x - 1$ following the instructions given under sketching linear functions.
- When the graphs are on the screen, to find the intersection point of the two lines, press SHIFT F1 and TRACE. The cursor will move along the line and give the coordinates at the bottom of the screen. Use the arrow keys to move the cursor along the lines. You may have to press the cursor many times before you see the little +.

- When you get close to the intersection point, zoom in to get a more accurate view by pressing [SHIFT] [F2] ZOOM IN [F3]. Move the cursor close to the point and zoom in as many times as needed. When you are on the exact spot, press [F1] to see the co-ordinates at the bottom of the screen.

Method 2: Elimination

This method is most useful when all variables have coefficients other than 1.

Example

Solve the following simultaneous equations by elimination.
(a) $4y + 5x = -2$ and
(b) $3y + 2x = 12$

Solution

Elimination involves putting the same coefficient in front of a chosen variable. Either variable can be chosen. Here the variable chosen is y.
(a) $\times 3 \Rightarrow 12y + 15x = -6$ The 3 is multiplied to every term to preserve equality.
(b) $\times 4 \Rightarrow 12y + 8x = 48$ There is now a common coefficient of 12 in front of the y.
Add or subtract the equations to eliminate the y. Here subtract to eliminate the $12y$.

$$12y + 15x = -6 \quad (a)$$
$$12y + 8x = 48 \quad (b)$$
(a) − (b) $7x = -54$

$$x = -\frac{54}{7}$$
$$= -7.71$$

Substitute this answer into the first equation: $4y + 5 \times -7.71 = -2$
$$4y = 36.55$$
$$y = 9.14$$

Answer is (−7.71, 9.14).

Method 3: Substitution

This method is most useful when a variable is isolated. In this question, y is isolated (on its own).

Example

Solve the following simultaneous equations by substitution.
(a) $y = 4x + 5$ and
(b) $3y + 2x = 12$

Solution

Substitute the expression $4x + 5$ for y into the second equation. Always use **brackets** for the substitution.

$$3y + 2x = 12$$
$$\Leftrightarrow 3(4x + 5) + 2x = 12 \quad \text{This is a linear equation and can be solved as such.}$$
$$\Leftrightarrow 12x + 15 + 2x = 12$$
$$\Leftrightarrow 14x = -3$$
$$\Leftrightarrow x = -\frac{3}{14}$$
$$= -0.21$$

Substitute this answer into the first equation: $y = 4x + 5$
$$y = 4 \times -0.21 + 5 = 4.14$$

Answer is (−0.21, 4.14).

A set of parallel lines

If the two lines are parallel, there will be no solution.

Example

Solve the following simultaneous equations by any method.
(a) $y = 5x + -2$ and
(b) $y = 5x + 8$

Solution

Eliminate y by subtracting the equations.
(a)–(b): $0 = 8 - -2$
$0 = 10$ *Not possible.*
These lines have no simultaneous solution. They are parallel.

An indeterminate system

If two lines are the same but expressed in different ways, there are an indeterminate number of solutions. This is because they have every point in common.

Example

Solve the following simultaneous equations by any method.
(a) $y = 5x + -2$ and
(b) $2y = 10x - 4$

Solution

(a) $\times 2 \Rightarrow 2y = 10x - 4$ (b)
Subtract (b) and (c) $0 = 0$ *Always true.*
These equations are indeterminate. They are the same line.

12 Non-linear functions

ALGEBRAIC FORMAT FOR NON-LINEAR FUNCTIONS

A non-linear function takes the form of $y = mx + c$. Below are some examples of non-linear functions and their graphs.

Cubics

- $y = -3x^3 + 5$ is a non-linear function since it has a term x^3.
- The graph confirms that the shape is not a straight line.
- This graph is called a **cubic** function.

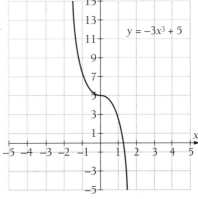

Hyperbolas

- $y = \dfrac{1}{x}$ is a non-linear function since it has a term x^{-1}.

  Note that $\dfrac{1}{x} = x^{-1}$.
- The graph confirms that the shape is not a straight line.
- This graph is called a **hyperbola**.

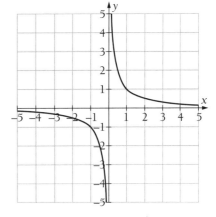

Quadratics

- $f(x) = x^2$ is a non-linear function since it has a term x^2.
- Ordered pairs that fit this function are given in the table of values.

  Plotting these ordered pairs on the cartesian plane gives a shape called a **parabola**, and its function is called a **quadratic equation**.
- The general form of a quadratic equation is $ax^2 + bx + c = 0$.

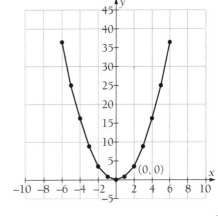

SOLVING QUADRATIC EQUATIONS

The general form of a quadratic equation is $ax^2 + bx + c = 0$. The **roots** or *zeros* of a quadratic equation are where the curve cuts the x-axis. To find these points is called solving for x.

Methods of solving quadratic equations

Method 1: The easiest quadratic
If $x^2 = a^2$, then $x = \pm a$.

Example
Find the roots of the equation $x^2 = 16$.

Solution
$x^2 = 4^2$
$x = \pm a$
$x = \pm 4$ Note: If the question is asked without the square, as in $\sqrt{16}$, the answer is just 4, not ± 4.
Also note: $\sqrt{-a}$ is not a real number.

Method 2: Using the graphics calculator

Example
Find the roots of the equation $2x^2 + 9x - 5 = 0$, using the graphics calculator (Casio 9850 GB Plus).

Solution

1. Press [EQUA] [EXE].

2. Press [POLYNOMIAL] [F2].

3. Press [F1] [2nd] [DEGREE].

4. Enter the values of a, b and c, pressing [EXE] after each entry: $a = 2$; $b = 9$; $c = -5$.

5. Press [F1] [SOLV].

The answers will appear in a table $\begin{matrix} 1 \\ 2 \end{matrix} \begin{bmatrix} 0.5 \\ -5 \end{bmatrix}$

Method 3: Factorisation
When solving by factorisation, the following rule is used: if $a \times b = 0$, either $a = 0$ or $b = 0$.

Example
Find the roots of the equation $2x^2 + 9x - 5 = 0$ by factorisation.

Solution
First factorise $ax^2 + bx + c$, using the method for trinomials (see p. 47).
$2x^2 + 9x - 5 = 0$
$= (2x - 1)(x + 5)$ See section on factorising trinomials (p. 47).
either $x + 5 = 0$ or $2x - 1 = 0$
$x = -5$ $x = \frac{1}{2}$

Method 4: Using the quadratic formula

If $ax^2 + bx + c = 0$, then $x = \dfrac{-b + \sqrt{b^2 - 4ac}}{2a}$ or $x = \dfrac{-b - \sqrt{b^2 - 4ac}}{2a}$

More concisely: $x = \dfrac{-b \pm \sqrt{b^2 - 4ac}}{2a}$

The **factors** of $ax^2 + bx + c$ are: $\left(x - \dfrac{-b + \sqrt{b^2 - 4ac}}{2a}\right)\left(x - \dfrac{-b - \sqrt{b^2 - 4ac}}{2a}\right)$

Example

Solve the equation $3x^2 - 7x - 6 = 0$ using the quadratic formula.

Solution

$3x^2 - 7x - 6 = 0$

Using the formula $a = 3$; $b = -7$; $c = -6$

$x = \dfrac{-b \pm \sqrt{b^2 - 4ac}}{2a}$

$x = \dfrac{--7 \pm \sqrt{49 - 4 \times 3 \times -6}}{2 \times 3}$

$x = \dfrac{7 \pm \sqrt{121}}{6}$

$x = \dfrac{7 + 11}{6}$ or $x = \dfrac{7 - 11}{6}$

$x = 3$ or $x = -0.67$

SKETCHING PARABOLAS

Using the graphics calculator to draw parabolas

Example

Sketch the function $y = 2 - 3x + x^2$ using the graphics calculator (Casio 9850).

Solution

First read the steps outlined for graphing linear functions using the graphics calculator on page 79.

1. Next to Y1 press [X, T] [X²] − 3 [X, T] + 2 [EXE].

2. Press [F6] [DRAW].

3. If a clear graph showing *x*- and *y*-intercepts does not appear on your screen, the view window needs adjustment.

    (a) First try the default view window settings—press [SHIFT] [F3] [F1].

    (b) Next try using zoom to get a clearer view. When the graph is on the screen, press [SHIFT] [F2] ZOOM OUT [F4]. You can repeat this as many times as needed to get the view you want.

    (c) If neither of these work, it may be necessary to calculate the roots of the equation using the formula

    $x = \dfrac{-b \pm \sqrt{b^2 - 4ac}}{2a}$. In this case, the answers are 1.5 and −0.25.

    The domain needs to include both of these values and the value 0, to show the *y*-intercept.

    Hence, set the *x*-values by pressing [SHIFT] [F3]: [Xmin]: −2

    [Xmax]: 4

Mathematics Dictionary Non-linear functions 89

4. If methods (a) or (b) were used to draw the parabola, the intercepts can be found by using trace and zoom.
    (a) While the graph is on the screen, press SHIFT F1 to trace along the function. Look at the co-ordinates at the bottom of the screen and use arrow keys to get the marker *close* to the value $x = 0$.
    (b) Press SHIFT F2 to zoom in on the spot. Press F3 IN. If you can't get exactly $x = 0$, repeat steps 1 and 2. The answer is $y = 1.5$. Repeat for other root.
5. Press EXIT.
6. Press MENU GRAPH EXE.

Features of a parabola

The coefficients a, b and c of the quadratic function $y = ax^2 + bx + c$ give information about the shape of the graph.

- If a is positive, the curve is **concave up**. When a curve is concave up it has a **minimum point** as marked.

- If a is negative, the curve is **concave down**. When a curve is concave down it has a **maximum point** as marked.

- The coefficient c gives information about the y-intercept: $(0, c)$ is where the curve cuts the y-axis.
- The **turning point** of the function occurs at $x = \frac{-b}{2a}$.
- The **roots** of the equation or the x-intercepts occur where the curve cuts the x-axis (i.e. where $y = 0$).

The discriminant

In the quadratic formula $\frac{-b \pm \sqrt{b^2 - 4ac}}{2a}$, the part under the square root sign is called the discriminant.

The discriminant gives information about the number of roots of a quadratic equation. The symbol for the discriminant is Δ. Hence, $\Delta = b^2 - 4ac$.

The discriminant can be positive, negative or zero.

1. $b^2 - 4ac < 0$
    When Δ is negative, it is not possible to find a real value for $\sqrt{b^2 - 4ac}$ since we cannot find the square root of a negative number. Hence, in this case there are *no real roots* of the quadratic equation and the parabola lies either completely above or below the x-axis.

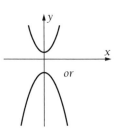

2. $b^2 - 4ac = 0$
    When $\Delta = 0$, $x = \frac{-b \pm 0}{2a} = \frac{-b}{2a}$ and so there is only *one root*.
    In this case the parabola would just touch the x-axis in one place.

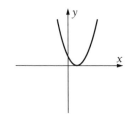

3. $b^2 - 4ac > 0$
   When Δ is positive, the parabola has *two real roots*.
   (a) If Δ is a perfect square (e.g. 4, 9, 16, 25), the roots are rational.
   (b) If Δ is not a perfect square, the roots are irrational.

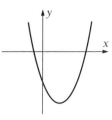

Example

Graph the quadratic equation $3x^2 - 7x - 6 = 0$ by analysis of its function.

Solution

$3x^2 - 7x - 6 = 0 \quad a = 3;\ b = -7;\ c = -6$

- The coefficient of the square term $a = 3$. This is positive and so the curve is concave up.
- The value of the constant term $c = -6$, so the y-intercept is $(0, -6)$.
- The quadratic equation $y = 3x^2 - 7x - 6$ has a turning point at $x = \frac{-b}{2a}$, $x = \frac{--7}{2 \times 3} = 1\frac{1}{6} = 1.167$.

  Since a is positive, this point is a minimum. Finding the y value for this $x = 1\frac{1}{6}$
  $$y = 3x^2 - 7x - 6$$
  $$= 3\left(1\frac{1}{6}\right)^2 - 7\left(1\frac{1}{6}\right) - 6$$
  $$= -10.083$$
  Hence, there is a minimum point at $(1.167, -10.083)$.
- Using the quadratic formula, the x-intercepts are $(-0.67, 0)$ and $(3, 0)$. The graph of the quadratic equation can now be drawn as shown.

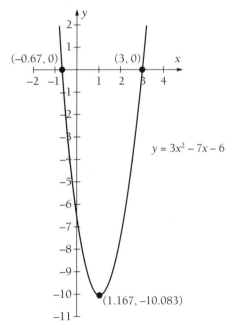

13 Interest

One way of saving money is to invest it in a financial institution and earn interest. **Interest** is a fee paid for the use of someone else's money. This money being used is called the **principal**. There are two kinds of interest—simple interest and compound interest.

SIMPLE INTEREST

Simple interest (or flat interest) is a fee paid at the end of the period of a loan. No interest payments are added in along the way to increase the principal and thus increase the interest. The formula for simple interest is:

$$I = P \times r \times t$$

where:
  P is the principal or the amount of money originally borrowed
  r is the rate per year (usually given as a percentage and so divided by 100)
  t is the time in years

Example

Find the simple interest on $5000 invested for 2 years at 13%.

Solution

$I = P \times r \times t$

$I = 5000 \times \dfrac{13}{100} \times 2$

$= \$1300$

For the following simple interest examples, the part of the question that requires *careful reading* is written in **bold**.

Example

Find the simple interest earned on $4000 invested for **18 months** at 5.5%.

Solution

$I = P \times r \times t$

$I = 4000 \times \dfrac{5.5}{100} \times \dfrac{18}{12}$ The 18 is divided by 12 because in the formula t is in years. There are 12 months in a year.

$= \$330$

Example

Find the simple interest earned on $1000 invested for 5 years at **2% per month.**

Solution

$I = P \times r \times t$

$I = 1000 \times \dfrac{24}{100} \times 5$ 2% per month means $2 \times 12 = 24\%$ per year.

$= \$1200$

Example

Sometimes we are asked to solve simple interest problems where we need to find something other than the interest. This involves rearranging the formula using algebra.

Find the interest rate if $5000 earns $250 over 2 years.

Solution

$$I = P \times r \times t$$
$$250 = 5000 \times r \times 2$$
$$\frac{250}{10\,000} = r$$
$$0.025 = r \text{ or } r = 2.5\%$$

Final amounts and monthly repayments

When simple interest is added to the original amount, the principal, the final amount is obtained.

$$\text{Final amount} = \text{Principal} + \text{Interest}$$
$$A = P + I$$

When an amount of money is borrowed at a flat interest rate, the monthly repayments or instalments are the amounts paid each month to repay the loan.

$$\text{Monthly instalments} = \frac{\text{Final amount}}{\text{Number of months}}$$

Example

Find the final amount that $6000 will grow into if invested for 8 years at 5.6%.

Solution

$$I = P \times r \times t$$
$$I = 6000 \times \frac{5.6}{100} \times 8$$
$$= \$2688$$
$$A = P + I$$
$$= \$6000 + \$2688$$
$$= \$8688$$

Example

Find the monthly instalments on $4000 borrowed for 2 years at 0.01% daily.

Solution

0.01% daily = 0.01 × 365% yearly = 10.95%

$$I = P \times r \times t$$
$$= \$4000 \times 10.95\% \times 2$$
$$= \$876$$
$$A = P + I$$
$$= \$4000 + \$876$$
$$= \$4876$$

$$\text{Monthly instalments} = \frac{\text{Final amount}}{\text{Number of months}}$$
$$= \frac{4786}{24}$$
$$= \$203.17 \text{ per month}$$

COMPOUND INTEREST

Compound interest differs from simple or flat interest in that interest payments are added in along the way to increase the principal. This, in turn, causes the interest to increase each period. A compound interest problem has the word compound in the question. The formula for compound interest is:

$$\text{Final amount: } A = P(1 + i)^n$$

where:

P = principal   *The original amount*
A = principal + interest   *The final amount*
n = the number of years of the loan × number of rest periods/year
i = interest rate (p.a.) as a decimal ÷ number of rest periods/year

The term *rest* is explained in the following table.

Word in question	Number of rests per year
yearly or annually	1
biannually, half yearly, semi-annually	2
quarterly	4
monthly	12
fortnightly	26
weekly	52
daily	365 or 366 if a leap year

Example

Find the final amount for $2000 invested at 12% compound interest for 5 years.

Solution

$P = \$2000; i = 0.12; n = 5$ *There is no statement of interest compounding over periods other than one year.*

$A = P(1 + i)^n$
$ = 2000(1 + 0.12)^5$ *Brackets are crucial for a correct calculator answer.*
$ = \$3524.68$

Example

Find the final amount for $2000 invested at 12% **compounding quarterly** for 5 years.

Solution

$P = \$2000; i = \frac{0.12}{4} = 0.03; n = 5 \times 4 = 20$ *There are four rests when compounding quarterly.*

$A = P(1 + i)^n$
$ = 2000(1 + 0.03)^{20}$ *Brackets are crucial for a correct calculator answer.*
$ = \$3612.22$

Example

Find the **final amount** for $2000 invested at 12% compounding daily for $1\frac{1}{2}$ years.

Solution

$P = \$2000; i = \frac{0.12}{365} = 0.000\,329; n = 1.5 \times 365 = 547.5$

$A = P(1 + i)^n$
$A = 2000(1 + 0.000\,329)^{547.5}$
$ = \$2394.36$

Examples involving algebra

With all of these examples it is best to avoid rounding off until the final answer.

Finding principal

Example

Find the **principal** invested if an amount of $2200 is achieved after 4 years, compounding weekly at 7%.

Solution

$A = \$2200$; $i = \dfrac{0.07}{52} = 0.00135$; $n = 4 \times 52 = 208$

$A = P(1 + i)^n$
$2200 = P(1 + 0.001\,35)^{208}$
$\$1663.04 = P$

Finding rate

Example:

If $8300 is invested for 2 years and compounds to $9500 with quarterly rests, what was the interest rate?

Solution

$A = \$9500$; $P = \$8300$; $n = 2 \times 4 = 8$
$A = P(1 + i)^n$
$9500 = 8300(1 + i)^8$
$\dfrac{9500}{8300} = (1 + i)^8$
$1.14 = (1 + i)^8$
$(1.14)^{\frac{1}{8}} = [(1 + i)^8]^{\frac{1}{8}}$ *Both sides are raised to the reciprocal exponent.*
$1.0165 = 1 + i$
$0.0165 = i$ is the rate per quarter; $0.0165 \times 4 = 0.0661$ or 6.61% is the rate per year.

Finding time

Example

How long will it take $5000 to grow to $8000 if interest is compounded monthly at 8.4%?

Solution

$A = \$8000$; $P = \$5000$; $i = \dfrac{0.084}{12} = 0.007$

$A = P(1 + i)^n$
$8000 = 5000(1 + 0.007)^n$
$\dfrac{8000}{5000} = 1.007^n$
$1.6 = 1.007^n$
$n = \log_{1.007} 1.6$
$n = \dfrac{\log 1.6}{\log 1.007}$ *Use the log button on your calculator.*
$n = 67.38$ months = about 5.6 years

14. Measurement

LENGTH

Units and conversions

Length is measured in kilometres (km), metres (m), centimetres (cm) and millimetres (mm).

$$km \xrightarrow{1000} m \xrightarrow{100} cm \xrightarrow{10} mm$$

$\rightarrow \times$
$\leftarrow \div$

To change to a smaller unit, multiply by the numbers between the units.
To change to a larger unit, divide by the numbers between the units.

Example

Convert the following:
(a) 13 mm to cm
(b) 1.4 km to m
(c) 25 000 cm to km

Solution

(a) 13 mm = 13 ÷ 10 cm
 = 1.3 cm
(b) 1.4 km = 1.4 × 1000 m
 = 1400 m
(c) 25 000 cm = 25 000 ÷ 100 000 km
 = 0.25 km

It takes 100 to convert from cm to m and 1000 to convert from m to km. Hence, it takes 100 × 1000 to convert from cm to km, so divide by 100 000.

Perimeter

Perimeter is the distance around a shape.

Perimeter of a rectangle

$P = 2l + 2w$
$P = 2(l + w)$

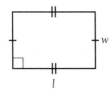

Example

Find the perimeter of the rectangle.

Solution

$P = 2(l + w)$
 $= 2(23 + 15)$
 $= 76$ mm

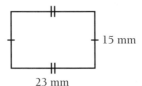

15 mm
23 mm

Perimeter of a square
$P = 4s$

Example
Find the perimeter of the square.

Solution
$P = 4s$
$ = 4 \times 15$
$ = 60$ km

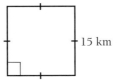

Perimeter of a parallelogram
$P = 2a + 2b$
$P = 2(a + b)$

Example
Find the perimeter of the parallelogram.

Solution
$P = 2(a + b)$
$ = 2(4 + 3)$
$ = 14$ mm

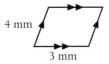

Perimeter of a triangle
$P = a + b + c$

Example
Find the perimeter of the triangle.

Solution
P = sum of the sides
$ = 1.1 + 1.1 + 1.8$
$ = 4$ m

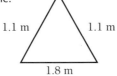

Circumference of a circle
$C = 2\pi r$ or πd Use the π button on your calculator.

Examples

Find the circumference of the circles.

(a)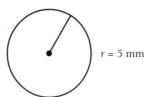

(b)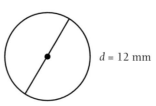

Solution

(a) $C = 2\pi r$
   $= 2\pi \times 5$
   $= 31.4$ mm

(b) $C = \pi d$
   $= \pi \times 12$
   $= 3.14 \times 12$
   $= 37.7$ mm

Perimeter of a sector (part of a circle)

$P = 2r + \dfrac{a°}{360°} \times 2\pi r$ The 2r part of the rule is the two radii. The rest of the rule is the perimeter of the sector curve.

Example

Find the perimeter of the sector.

Solution

$P = 2r + \dfrac{a°}{360°} \times 2\pi r$

$= 2 \times 10 + \dfrac{70}{360} \times 2\pi \times 10$

$= 32.22$ cm

Perimeters with algebra

Example

Find the perimeter of the triangle.

Solution

$P = 3d + 3d + 4d$
$= 10d$ Since we do not know the value of d, this is the final answer.

Example

The perimeter of this triangle is 40 cm. Find the length of each side.

Solution
$P = 3d + 3d + 4d$
$ = 10d$
Given: $P = 40$ cm
$\therefore 10d = 40$
$d = 4$ cm
The length of sides $3d = 3 \times d$
$ = 3 \times 4$ cm
$ = 12$ cm
The length of side $4d = 4 \times d$
$ = 4 \times 4$ cm
$ = 16$ cm

AREA

Units and conversions

Area is the space inside a shape. Area is measured in square kilometres (km^2), hectares (ha), square metres (m^2), square centimetres (cm^2) and square millimetres (mm^2).

$$km^2 \;{}^{100}\; ha \;{}^{10000}\; m^2 \;{}^{10000}\; cm^2 \;{}^{100}\; mm^2$$

$\rightarrow \times$
$\leftarrow \div$

To change to a smaller unit, multiply by the numbers between the units.
To change to a larger unit, divide by the numbers between the units.

Example

Convert the following:
(a) $2.5\ m^2$ to cm^2
(b) $10\ 050\ mm^2$ to m^2

Solution
(a) $2.5\ m^2 = 2.5 \times 10\ 000\ cm^2$
$ = 25\ 000\ cm^2$
(b) $10\ 050\ mm^2 = 10\ 050 \div 1\ 000\ 000\ m^2$
$ = 0.010\ 05\ m^2$

Area of a rectangle

$A = l \times w$

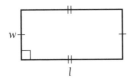

Example

Find the area of this rectangle.

Solution

$A = l \times w$
$= 230 \times 180$
$= 41\,400$ mm²

180 mm
230 mm

This is not a sensible unit for such a large measure.
41 400 mm² = 41 400 ÷ 100 cm² = 414 cm²

Area of a square

$A = s^2$

s

Example

Find the area of this square.

Solution

$A = s^2$
$= 1.07^2$
$= 1.1449$ km²

1.07 km

Area of a parallelogram

$A = b \times h$

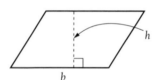
h
b

Example

Find the area of this parallelogram.

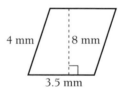
4 mm   8 mm
3.5 mm

Solution

$A = b \times h$
$= 8 \times 3.5$ *Always look for the two measures that meet at a right angle.*
$= 28$ mm²

Area of a triangle

$A = \frac{1}{2}(b \times h)$

h
b

h
b

Example

Find the area of this triangle.

Solution

First convert 120 mm to cm.

120 mm = 120 ÷ 10 cm
 = 12 cm

Area = $\frac{1}{2}(b \times h)$

 = $\frac{1}{2}(12 \times 21.3)$ *Again choose the two measures that meet at a right angle.*

 = 127.8 cm²

Area of a circle

$A = \pi r^2$

Example

Find the area of the circle.

Solution

Area = πr^2

 = 3.14 × 0.5 × 0.5

 = 0.785 mm²   *Notice we divided the diameter by 2 to get the radius.*

$d = 1$ mm

Area of a circle sector (part of a circle)

$A = \frac{a°}{360°} \times \pi r^2$

Example

Find the area of the following circle sectors.

(a)   10 cm, 75°

(b) $r = 24$ mm, 89°

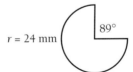

Solution

(a) $A = \frac{a°}{360°} \times \pi r^2$

 = $\frac{75}{360} \times \pi \times 100$

 = 65.45 cm²

(b)   This time we are given the angle in the acute angle. Therefore, the angle in the required major sector = 360° − 89° = 271°.

$A = \frac{a°}{360°} \times \pi r^2$

 = $\frac{271}{360} \times \pi \times 24 \times 24$

 = 1362.19 mm²

Area of a trapezium

$A = \frac{1}{2}h(a + b)$ Note: a and b are always the two parallel edges.

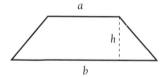

Example

Find the area of this trapezium.

Solution
$A = \frac{1}{2}h(a + b)$
$= 0.5 \times 10 \times 26$
$= 130 \text{ m}^2$

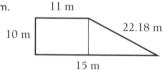

Areas of combined shapes and shapes embedded in other shapes

Often calculations determining the area of real-life shapes involve finding the area of **combined shapes**. Combined shapes are formed when shapes are joined together.

Another situation involves finding the area of shapes that lie inside other shapes. Such shapes are said to be **embedded**.

These problems are best approached by considering examples.

Example

Find the area of the following shapes.

(a)
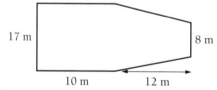

(b)
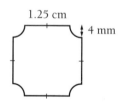

Solution

(a)   This is an example of a combined shape, so the areas are added together.
Area of the rectangle $= l \times b$
$= 10 \times 17$
$= 170 \text{ m}^2$

Area of trapezium $= \frac{(a + b)}{2} \times h$
$= \frac{(8 + 17)}{2} \times 12$ 8 and 17 are the lengths of the two parallel edges of the trapezium.
$= 150 \text{ m}^2$

Total area $= 170 + 150$
$= 320 \text{ m}^2$

(b)   This is an example of an embedded shape so we find the area of the outside square and take away the four quarter circles (in the corners).
First convert all measures to the same unit:
$1.25 \text{ cm} = 1.25 \times 10 = 12.5 \text{ mm}$
Area of outside square $= s^2$
$= (12.5 + 2 \times 4)^2$
$= 420.25 \text{ mm}^2$

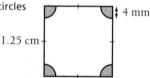

Area of the 4 quarter circles = area of one whole circle
= πr^2
= $\pi \times 4^2$
= 50.27 mm²
Hence, required area = 420.25 − 50.27
= 369.98 mm²

SURFACE AREA

Most solids can be made by folding a two-dimensional shape, called a **net**. The **surface area** of a solid is the sum of the areas of the faces of this net.

Surface area of all prisms = Area of the (top + bottom + sides)

The surface area of a prism can also be expressed in the same way for all prisms:

Surface area = 2 × Area of base + Perimeter of base × Height

Both of these approaches are outlined below.

Cube

Net

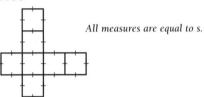

All measures are equal to s.

Surface area of a cube

SA = 2 × Area of base + Perimeter of base × Height
= $2s^2 + 4 \times s \times s$
SA = $6s^2$

Surface area of a **cube by net**
SA = Area of the (top + bottom + sides)
= $s^2 + s^2 + s^2 + s^2 + s^2 + s^2$
SA = $6s^2$

Example

Find the surface area of this cube

Solution
SA = $6s^2$
= $6 \times 5 \times 5$
= 150 cm²

5 cm

Rectangular-based prism

Net

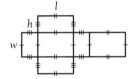

Surface area of a rectangular-based prism

SA = 2 × Area of base + Perimeter of base × Height
SA = $2 \times l \times w + 2(l + w) \times h$

Surface area of a **rectangular-based prism by net**
SA = Area of 6 rectangular faces
   = lw + lw + lh + lh + wh + wh
   = 2lw + 2lh + 2wh

Example

Find the surface area of this rectangular prism.

Solution
SA = 2 × l × w + 2(l + w) × h
   = 2 × 10 × 4 + 2(10 + 4) × 5
   = 220 cm²

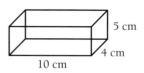

Cylinder

Net

Surface area of a cylinder
SA = 2 × Area of base + Perimeter of base × Height
SA = $2\pi r^2 + 2\pi r \times h$
Surface area of a **cylinder by net**
SA = Area of the (circle top, bottom + sides)
SA = $2 \times \pi r^2 + 2\pi r \times h$

Example

Find the surface area of this cylinder.

Solution
SA = $2\pi r^2 + 2\pi r \times h$
   = $2\pi \times 5^2 + 2\pi \times 5 \times 10$
   = 471.24 mm²

r = 5 mm   h = 10 mm

Triangular-based prism

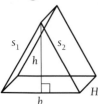

Net

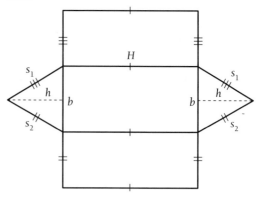

Surface area of a triangular-based prism
SA = 2 × Area of base + Perimeter of base × Height
   = $2\left(\dfrac{b \times h}{2}\right)$ + (sum of the sides) × H
SA = b × h + (sum of the sides) × H

Surface area of a **triangular-based prism by net**
SA = Area of the base and top + Area of sides
   = $2 \times \frac{1}{2}h \times b + b \times H + s_1 \times H + s_2 \times H$
   = $h \times b + b \times H + s_1 \times H + s_2 \times H$

Example

Find the surface area of this triangular-based prism.

Solution

$$SA = h \times b + (\text{sum of the sides}) \times h$$
$$= 4 \times 6 + (6 + 5 + 5) \times 2$$
$$= 4 \times 6 + 6 \times 2 + 5 \times 2 + 5 \times 2$$
$$= 56 \text{ m}^2$$

Trapezoidal prism

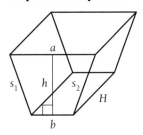

Net (not to scale)

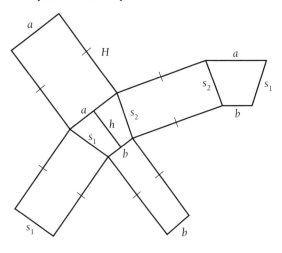

Surface area of a trapezium-based prism

$$SA = 2 \times \text{Area of base} + \text{Perimeter of base} \times \text{Height}$$
$$= 2 \times \frac{(s_1 + s_2) \times h}{2} + (\text{sum of the sides}) \times H$$
$$SA = (s_1 + s_2) \times h + (\text{sum of the sides}) \times H$$

Surface area of a **trapezium-based prism by net**

$$SA = \text{Area of the two trapezium ends} + \text{Area of sides}$$
$$= 2\frac{(a+b)}{2}h + a \times H + b \times H + s_1 \times H + s_2 \times H$$
$$SA = (a + b) \times h + a \times H + b \times H + s_1 \times H + s_2 \times H$$

Example

Find the surface area of this trapezoidal prism.

Solution

$$\text{Surface area} = (s_1 + s_2) \times h + (\text{sum of the sides}) \times H$$
$$= (8 + 11) \times 4 + (8 + 11 + 5 + 5) \times 3$$
$$= 163 \text{ cm}^2$$

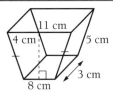

MASS

Units and conversions

The **mass** of an object is the amount of matter it contains. Mass is measured in tonnes (t), kilograms (kg), grams (g) and milligrams (mg). The difference between mass and weight is that weight changes depending on your distance from the Earth's centre. Your weight on Earth is different to your weight on the Moon. Your mass remains unchanged.

Conversion between units of mass is given below:

---

tonnes $\xrightarrow{1000}$ **kg** $\xrightarrow{1000}$ **g** $\xrightarrow{1000}$ **mg**

→ ×
← ÷

To change to a smaller unit, multiply by the number between the units.
To change to a larger unit, divide by the number between the units.

Example

Find the total mass of 500 nails each weighing 1.9 grams.

Solution

Mass = (1.9 × 500) grams
= 950 grams
= 0.95 kg

CAPACITY

Units and conversions

Capacity is the quantity of fluid (liquid or gas) that the shape will hold. Capacity is measured in kilolitres (kL), litres (L) and millilitres (mL). These units are linked to the units for volume: cm^3 and m^3.

In summary, the *links* between *volume* and *capacity* are:

$$1\ cm^3 \leftrightarrow 1\ mL$$
$$1000\ cm^3 \leftrightarrow 1\ L$$
$$1\ m^3 \leftrightarrow 1\ kL$$

Example

What capacity has a swimming pool of dimension 50 000 m^3?

Solution

50 000 m^3 = 50 000 kL

Conversion between units of capacity is given below:

kL $\xrightarrow{1000}$ L $\xrightarrow{1000}$ mL

→ ×
← ÷

To change to a smaller unit, multiply by the number between the units.
To change to a larger unit, divide by the number between the units.

Example

How many mL in a 1.25 L bottle of shampoo?

Solution

1.25 L = 1.25 × 1000 mL
= 1250 mL

VOLUME

Units

The **volume** of a solid is the amount of space it takes up. Volume is measured in cubic kilometres (km^3), cubic metres (m^3), cubic centimetres (cm^3) and cubic millimetres (mm^3).

Volume of a right prism

The rule for finding the volume of a right prism can be defined in the same way for all prisms.

$$\text{Volume of prism} = \text{Area of base} \times \text{Height}$$

Volume of a cube

V = Area of base × Height
   = $s \times s \times s$
$V = s^3$

Example

Find the volume and capacity of this cube.

Solution
$V = s^3$
  = 5^3
  = 125 cm³
Capacity: 1 cm³ = 1 mL
           125 cm³ = 125 mL

5 cm

Volume of a rectangular-based prism

V = Area of base × Height
$V = l \times w \times h$

Example

Find the volume and capacity of this rectangular-based prism.

Solution
$V = lwh$
  = 10 × 4 × 5
  = 200 mm³
Capacity: 1 cm³ = 1 mL
           200 mm³ = 0.2 cm³
           0.2 cm³ = 0.2 mL

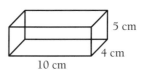

Volume of a triangular-based prism

V = Area of base × Height
$V = \dfrac{h \times b}{2} \times H$

Example

Find the volume and capacity of this triangular-based prism.

Solution
$V = \dfrac{h \times b}{2} H$
  = $\dfrac{10 \times 8}{2} \times 4$
  = 160 m³
Capacity: 1000 m³ = 1 kL
          160 m³ = 0.16 kL

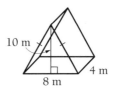

Volume of a cylinder

V = Area of base × Height
$V = \pi r^2 h$

Mathematics Dictionary **Measurement**

Example

Find the surface area of this cylinder.

Solution

$V = \pi r^2 h$
$= \pi \times 5 \times 5 \times 10$
$= 785.4 \text{ mm}^3$
$= 0.7854 \text{ cm}^3$

$r = 5$ mm
$h = 10$ mm

VOLUME AND SURFACE AREA OF PYRAMIDS

The cone has one-third of the volume of the cylinder with the same base and height.

The volume of a pyramid $= \frac{1}{3}$ Area of the base $\times$ Height

Volume and surface area rules for pyramids are outlined below.

Volume of a square-based pyramid

$V = \frac{1}{3}s^2 h$

Example

Find the volume and surface area of this square-based pyramid.

Solution

$V = \frac{1}{3}s^2 h$
$ = \frac{1}{3} \times 9 \times 10$
$ = 30 \text{ mm}^3$

$SA = s^2 + 4 \times \frac{sh}{2}$
$ = s^2 + 2sh$
$ = 3 \times 3 + 2 \times 3 \times 10$
$ = 69 \text{ mm}^2$

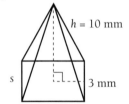

$h = 10$ mm
s
3 mm

Volume of a cone

$V = \frac{1}{3}\pi r^2 h$

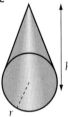

Example

Find the volume and surface area of this cone.

Solution

$V = \frac{1}{3}\pi r^2 h$
$ = \frac{1}{3}\pi \times 7 \times 7 \times 11$
$ = 564.44 \text{ m}^3$

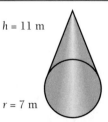

$h = 11$ m
$r = 7$ m

$$SA = \pi rs + \pi r^2$$
$$= \pi \times 7 \times 12 + \pi \times 7 \times 7$$
$$= 417.83 \text{ m}^2$$

Volume of a triangular-based pyramid (tetrahedron)

$$V = \tfrac{1}{3} \times \tfrac{1}{2} \times h \times H$$
$$= \tfrac{1}{6} \times b \times h \times H$$

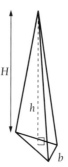

Example

Find the volume and surface area of this triangular-based pyramid.
Slant height of front face is 13 mm; of side face is 12.5 mm and of back face is 12.2 mm.

$H = 12$ mm

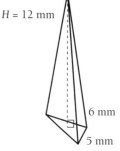

Solution

$$V = \tfrac{1}{6} \times b \times h \times H$$
$$= \tfrac{1}{6} \times 6 \times 5 \times 12$$
$$= 72 \text{ mm}$$

Surface area = Sum of the areas of four triangles

SA of base triangle $= \tfrac{1}{2} \times 5 \times 6 = 15$ mm²

SA of other three triangles: $\tfrac{1}{2} \times 6 \times 13 = 39$ mm²

$$\tfrac{1}{2} \times 5 \times 12.5 = 31.25 \text{ mm}^2$$

$$\tfrac{1}{2} \times \sqrt{6^2 + 5^2} \times 12.2 = 20.23 \text{ mm}^2$$

Total SA $= 15 + 39 + 31.25 + 20.23$
$= 105.48$ mm²

Surface area of a sphere

$SA = 4\pi r^2$

Example

Find the surface area of this sphere.

$r = 7$ m

Solution
$$SA = 4\pi r^2$$
$$= 4 \times \pi \times 7 \times 7$$
$$= 615.75 \text{ m}^2$$

Volume of a sphere

$V = \tfrac{4}{3}\pi r^3$

Example

Find the volume of this sphere.

$r = 7$ m

Solution
$$V = \tfrac{4}{3}\pi r^3$$
$$= \tfrac{4}{3}\pi \times 7^3$$
$$= 1436.76 \text{ m}^3$$

Surface area of an open hemisphere

$SA = 2\pi r^2$

Example

Find the surface area of this open hemisphere.

Solution

$SA = 2\pi r^2$
$= 2 \times \pi \times 7 \times 7$
$= 307.88 \text{ m}^2$

$r = 7$ m

Surface area of a closed hemisphere (with a lid)

$SA = 3\pi r^2$

Example

Find the surface area of this closed hemisphere.

Solution

$SA = 3\pi r^2$
$= 3 \times \pi \times 49$
$= 461.81 \text{ m}^2$

$r = 7$ m

15 Right-angled triangles

A **right-angled triangle** is one with a 90° angle. The side opposite this angle is called the **hypotenuse**. The hypotenuse is always the *longest side* in a right-angled triangle.

Right-angled triangles have special properties that allow us to find the measures of sides and angles from other known measures within the triangle. One such property is called the **Theorem of Pythagoras**, named after the famous mathematician who discovered it.

THEOREM OF PYTHAGORAS

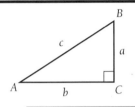

$$c^2 = a^2 + b^2$$

In any right-angled triangle, the square of the hypotenuse equals the sum of the squares on the other two sides.

This property can be used to find missing sides in right-angled triangles.

Example

Find the unknown in the following triangles.

(a)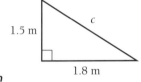

(b)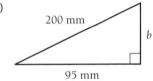

Solution

(a) The unknown is the hypotenuse.
$c^2 = a^2 + b^2$
$c^2 = 1.8^2 + 1.5^2$
$c^2 = 3.24 + 2.25$
$c^2 = 5.49$
$c = 2.34$ m

(b) The unknown is not the hypotenuse.
$c^2 = a^2 + b^2$
$200^2 = 95^2 + b^2$
$40\,000 = 9025 + b^2$
$40\,000 - 9025 = b^2$
$30\,975 = b^2$
176 mm $= b$

NAMING THE SIDES IN A RIGHT-ANGLED TRIANGLE

In any right-angled triangle the sides have special names. The hypotenuse is always the longest side. The *opposite* side is the side *away* from the right angle and the *adjacent* side is *close* to the right angle. *Note*: Always name the hypotenuse first.

The sides which are adjacent and opposite change depending on the position of the angle.

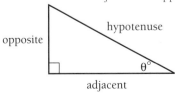

The angle opposite a is θ.
The angle adjacent to a is σ.

Example

For this triangle name the hypotenuse, the opposite side and adjacent side to the angle marked θ.

Solution
hypotenuse = AC
adjacent side = AB
opposite side = BC

THE TANGENT RATIO IN A RIGHT-ANGLED TRIANGLE

In a right-angled triangle

$$\tan \theta = \frac{\text{opposite}}{\text{adjacent}}$$

This ratio is the same regardless of the size of the triangle.

Example

Find the tan of θ in this triangle.

Solution

$\tan \theta = \frac{\text{opposite}}{\text{adjacent}}$

$= \frac{1.8}{2.5}$

$= 0.7$

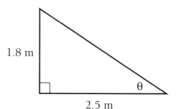

Finding tan ratios with the calculator

Because tan θ is constant, regardless of the size of the triangle, mathematicians have compiled tables for the tangent ratio of all different angles. We will only consider the angles between 0° and 90°. The tangent ratio for all of these angles have been programmed into your calculator. Make sure your calculator is in degree mode. It should say 'Deg' at the top of the screen.

Example

(a) Find the tan of this angle using your calculator.
(b) Check that this answer is the same as when using the formula:

$\tan \theta = \frac{\text{opposite}}{\text{adjacent}}$

Solution
(a) **Calculator steps:** [tan] 14° = 0.25
(b) tan 14° = $\frac{1}{4}$ = 0.25

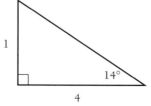

Example

Find the angle θ, to the nearest whole degree, if tan θ = 0.75.

Solution:
Calculator steps: [2nd F] [tan] 0.75 = 37°

Finding unknown angles and sides

In a right-angled triangle, missing sides and angles can be found using the equation for $\tan \theta = \frac{\text{opposite}}{\text{adjacent}}$, and calculator values for the tangent of angles.

Example

Find x in the following.

(a) 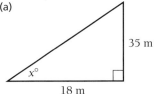 (b) 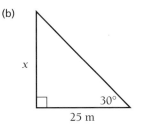 (c)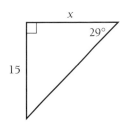

Solution

(a) $\tan x° = \frac{\text{opposite}}{\text{adjacent}}$

$\tan x° = \frac{35}{18}$

$x = \tan^{-1} \frac{35}{18}$

$x = 62.78°$

Use the $\boxed{2^{\text{nd}} \text{F}}$ $\boxed{\tan}$ and $\boxed{a^{b}/c}$ buttons on your calculator

(b) $\tan \theta° = \frac{\text{opposite}}{\text{adjacent}}$

$\tan 30° = \frac{x}{25}$

$0.58 = \frac{x}{25}$

$x = 0.58 \times 25$

$x = 14.5$ m

(c) $\tan \theta = \frac{\text{opposite}}{\text{adjacent}}$

$\tan 29° = \frac{15}{x}$

$0.555 = \frac{15}{x}$

$\frac{0.555}{1} = \frac{15}{x}$ Cross-multiply.

$0.555 \times x = 15 \times 1$

$x = \frac{15}{0.555}$

$x = 27$

Angles of elevation and depression

- An **angle of elevation** goes *out* and *up*.

- An **angle of depression** goes *out* and *down*.

Example

The angle of elevation from the signpost to the top of the tree is 67°. The signpost is 15 m away. How high is the tree?

Solution

$\tan 67° = \frac{x}{15}$

$2.36 = \frac{x}{15}$

$2.36 \times 15 = x$

$35.34 = x$

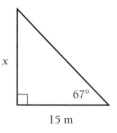

Example

The angle of depression from a lighthouse to a boat is 15°. If the lighthouse is 30 m high, how far away is the boat?

Solution

$\tan 15° = \frac{30}{x}$

$0.27 = \frac{30}{x}$

$0.27x = 30$

$x = \frac{30}{0.27}$

$x = 111.11$ m

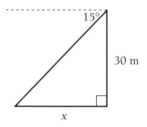

SINE (SIN) AND COSINE (COS) RATIOS

The sine and cosine ratios also apply to right-angled triangles.

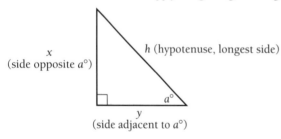

$\sin a° = \frac{\text{opposite}}{\text{hypotenuse}} = \frac{x}{h}$

$\cos a° = \frac{\text{adjacent}}{\text{hypotenuse}} = \frac{y}{h}$

The following are some examples of the use of sine and cosine ratios.

Example

Find x.

Solution

$\sin 30° = \frac{\text{opposite}}{\text{hypotenuse}}$

$\sin 30° = \frac{x}{25}$

$0.5 = \frac{x}{25}$ Use the $\boxed{\sin}$ button on your calculator to get 0.5.

$0.5 \times 25 = x$ Make sure your calculator is in degrees.

12.5 m $= x$

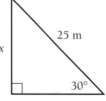

Example

Find x.

Solution

$\sin x° = \dfrac{\text{opposite}}{\text{hypotenuse}}$

$\sin x° = \dfrac{15}{25}$

$x = \sin^{-1} \dfrac{15}{25}$ Use the [2nd F] [sin] and [a b/c] buttons on your calculator.

$x = 36.87°$

Example

Find x.

Solution

$\cos 30° = \dfrac{\text{adjacent}}{\text{hypotenuse}}$

$\cos 30° = \dfrac{25}{x}$

$0.866 = \dfrac{25}{x}$

$0.866x = 25$

$x = \dfrac{25}{0.866}$

$x = 28.87$ m   On the calculator press [cos] 30 [=].

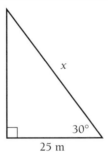

Example

Find x.

Solution

$\cos x° = \dfrac{\text{adjacent}}{\text{hypotenuse}}$

$\cos x° = \dfrac{18}{25}$

$x = \cos^{-1} \dfrac{18}{25}$

$x = 4.395°$ Use the [2nd F] [cos] and [a b/c] buttons on your calculator.

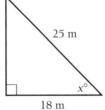

16 Earth geometry

THE COORDINATE SYSTEM FOR MAPS

Position on the Earth is defined by using lines of **latitude** and **longitude**.
   Parallels (or lines) of latitude are small circles measured *parallel* to the Equator, as shown opposite.

Latitude lines: Parallel to Equator.

Lines of latitude are measured north (N) and south (S) of the Equator and run east to west.

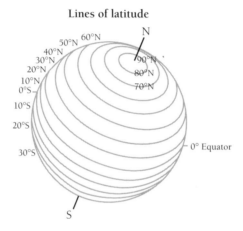

Lines of latitude

   Lines of longitude are circles that pass through the North and South Poles. Lines of longitude are the longest circles. They are all the *same* size and run north and south. Each line of longitude is broken in half to make two **meridians**. The central (prime) meridian goes through Greenwich, near London, and all the others are either east (E) or west (W) of this one.

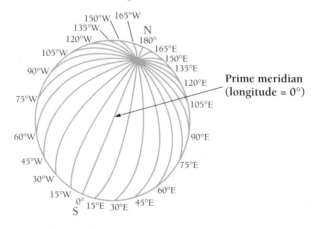

Lines of longitude

Thus, position on the Earth is defined as an ordered pair using the latitude and longitude.

Position = latitude, longitude

The unit used to measure latitude and longitude is degrees. The symbol for degree is °.

Latitude runs from 0° at the Equator to 90°N or 90°S at the poles. Latitude is the *first* co-ordinate given: (33°N, ___) or (43°S, ___).

Longitude runs from 0° at the prime meridian to 180° east or west, halfway around the globe. Longitude is the *second* co-ordinate given (___, 11°E) or (___, 59°W).

DISTANCES BETWEEN PLACES ON THE SAME LONGITUDE

Each **degree of latitude** on the same meridian of longitude equals approximately *111 km*. Hence, to travel from one place to another on the same meridian of longitude = 111 km × latitude degree difference between the two locations.

To find the degree difference between two locations:
- when locations are on *opposite* sides of the Equator, the degree measures are **added**
- when locations are on the *same* side of the Equator, the degree measures are **subtracted**

Example

Find the distance between Cape Town (34°S, 19°E) and Budapest (47°N, 19°E).

Solution

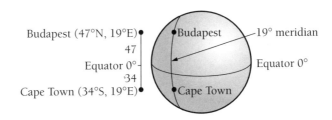

Since Budapest is north and Cape Town is south, they are on *opposite* sides of the Equator, so we need to **add**: 34° + 47° = 81°.

Hence, the distance is: 81° × 111 = 8991 km.   *Remember, each degree on the same meridian = 111 km.*

Example

Find the distance between *A* (50°N, 50°E) and *B* (75°N, 50°E).

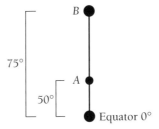

Solution

Since these two cities are both on the same side of the Equator, we need to **subtract**:
75° − 50° = 25°.
Hence, the distance is 25° × 111 = 2775 km.

DISTANCES BETWEEN PLACES ON THE SAME LATITUDE

When finding the distance between two places on the same latitude, the rule is:

$$\frac{d°}{360°} \times 40\,000 \times \cos\theta$$ where $d°$ is the difference in longitude and θ is the line of latitude

Example

Find the distance between A (30°N, 100°E) and B (30°N, 40°E).

Solution

A (30°N, 100°E) and B (30°N, 40°E) are both on the *same* side of the Greenwich meridian (they are both east), so we subtract the degrees: 100° − 40° = 60°   *Note: If they were on different sides, add.*

Distance $= \left(\frac{60}{360} \times 40\,000\right) \times \cos 30° = 5773.5$ km

BEARINGS AND COMPASS POINTS

The **compass points**—north, south, east and west—can be used to define direction.

Direction can be made clearer by using more compass points—north-east, north-west, south-east and south-west.

A **bearing** is an angle measured from one point to another in a clockwise direction. **True bearings** are directions given with reference to the compass direction *north*.

To find a bearing from *A* to *B*

Example

(a) Find the true bearing from A to B.   (b) Find the true bearing from B to A.

Solution

(a) 1. Draw a line north through the letter that comes after the word 'from'—in this case A.
    2. Draw a line connecting A and B.
    3. Measure the angle created. The angle is 80°.

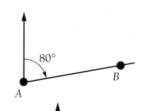

(b) 1. Draw a line north through B.
    2. Draw a line connecting A and B.
    3. Measure the angle created. It is 260°.

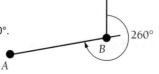

17 Data

TYPES OF DATA

Data is information that is collected. It can be **discrete** or **continuous**.
Continuous data is data which is measured and has meaning between the scores. Some examples of continuous data include:
- heights of students in a class   *It is meaningful to say that a student's height is 85 cm or 86 cm, but it is also meaningful to say that a student is 85.36 cm tall.*
- lengths of javelin throws
- time taken to complete a task

Discrete data is counted and has no meaning between the scores. Discrete data can also be **categorical**, that is, it divides items into categories. Some examples of discrete data are:
- the number of socks purchased at the uniform shop—the data along both axes are discrete numbers. *There might be 120 pairs of socks sold or 121 pairs, but it is not meaningful to say that there are 120.5 pairs of socks sold.*
- placing vehicles into categories (2 wheels, cars, trucks, caravans) for payment at a toll booth—the data along one axis would be categorical (2 wheels, cars, trucks, caravans) and along the other axis discrete numbers

PROPERTIES OF GRAPHS

The purpose of graphs is to display data clearly so it is easier to understand. **Trends**, or patterns, in data that show some pattern, are then more easily noted.
- All graphs should have a **title**.
- Graphs are bound by **axes** which form a framework for the graph. These axes must be named.
- All graphs have **variables** or factors which impact upon the data. These might include age, time, distance or income.
- The **scale** of a graph refers to the positioning of points along the axes at set distances. The scale is chosen for clarity and accuracy.

Line graphs

In **line graph**s, data along both axes is **continuous**. *Two* sources of data are shown. Line graphs are used for prediction. The following is an example of a line graph.

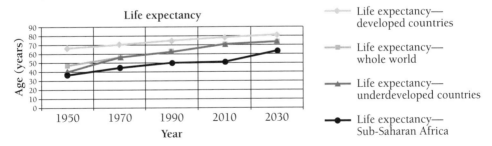

Bar or column graphs

Bar or **column graphs** are used when *discrete* information is given in amounts or *frequencies* of a set of categories. The bars have *equal widths* and *equal gaps*. Bars are usually vertical, but may be horizontal.

The following bar graph shows items sold at the school uniform shop, which relates to the information in the table.

Steps for drawing a bar graph with the Casio graphics calculator

1. Press MENU STAT and enter information into List 1 using arrow keys and EXE.

2. Press F1 GRPH F6 SET.

3. Check that the title is StatGraph 1.

4. Under G-Type, for graph type, choose histogram. You may have to use the arrow at F6 to see all choices.

5. Press XList F1 List 1.

6. Press Freq: 1

7. Press EXIT.

8. Press F1 GPH1.

Compound graphs

The above information is now divided into sales for boys and girls as shown in this table. This information is well displayed in a **compound bar graph**, or a **split bar graph**.

Item	Sales (girls)	Sales (boys)
Hats	281	295
Shirts	1112	0
Pants	0	2136
Socks	1564	1786
Skirts	443	0

Split bar graph

A **split bar graph** can be used when *comparisons* are needed within a category. In this example, the number of uniform items purchased by students has been split to show the number purchased by boys and the number purchased by girls.

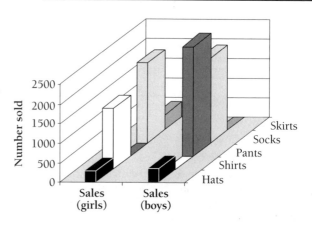

Divided bar graph

In a **divided bar graph**, the information is displayed in bars with the categories on top of each other so that they add to make the whole.

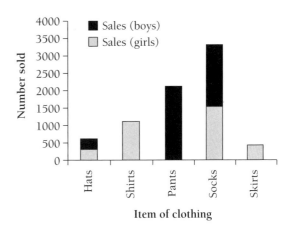

Histograms

Histograms and **stem and leaf plots** are used for **continuous** data when the *frequencies* of particular categories are being compared. The areas of the bars of a histogram are in proportion to the corresponding frequencies. Information is arranged so that there is *no overlap* of categories. For example, if the first category is 60–69, then the next must be 70–79 and *not* 69–79.

Example

The height of seedlings, measured to the nearest whole mm, are: 63, 82, 70, 87, 84, 76, 75, 78, 88, 104, 96, 75, 92, 86, 119, 82, 85, 78, 89, 87. Draw a histogram of the data.

Solution

1. Arrange the data in a frequency distribution table.

Height (mm)	Frequency
60–69	1
70–79	6
80–89	9
90–99	2
100–109	1
110–119	1

2. Draw the histogram with categories 59.5–69.5, 69.5–79.5 etc because the data is *continuous*. This means that a measure of 59.7, which would round up to 60, will be included in the 60–69 category.

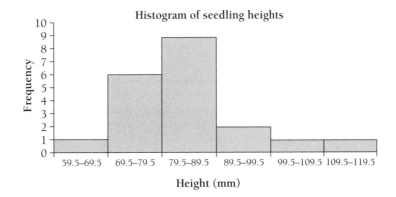

Mathematics Dictionary **Data**

A frequency polygon

When the *midpoints* of the tops of the bars of a histogram are joined, a **frequency polygon** is formed. An example is shown here.

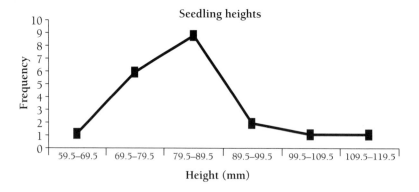

Stem and leaf plots

A **stem and leaf plot** differs from a histogram in that it includes both *detail* and *general formation*. Detail is given because all the scores are listed for view. The formation is given in that the shape of the stem and leaf plot is the same as a side on view of a histogram. This means that a quick glance gives an impression of the spread of data. The scores used in this stem and leaf plot are those from the histogram example above.

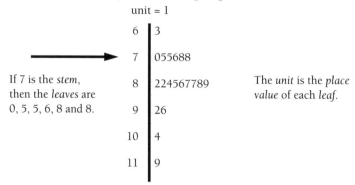

If 7 is the *stem*, then the *leaves* are 0, 5, 5, 6, 8 and 8.

The *unit* is the *place value* of each *leaf*.

Frequency distribution tables

One way of organising information is to put it in a **frequency distribution table**. In these tables, tally marks are used to count the frequency of particular responses.

Example

A school has raised $50 000 to enhance student facilities. Students were surveyed as to what would be their preference for spending a grant of money for their school: a recording studio, a media lounge, sports equipment; shaded outdoor facilities with comfortable furniture, or hire a well-known band for a school party. The results are listed below in a frequency distribution table.

Choice of facility	Tally	Frequency
Recording studio	///	3
Media lounge	//// //	7
Sports equipment	//// ////	9
Shaded outdoor facilities with comfortable furniture	//// //// //	12
Hire a well-known band for a school party	////	5
Total		36

(a) How many students were surveyed?
(b) How many students wanted a media lounge?
(c) How many students wanted some form of music facility?
(d) What was the most popular choice?

Solution
(a) 36 students (b) 7 (c) 3 + 7 + 5 = 15 (d) Outdoor facilities

Circle graphs (pie graph)

A **circle graph**, like a bar graph, displays amounts or frequencies of a set of categories. It differs from a bar or column graph in that the categories combine to make a *meaningful whole*, which is usually the name of the graph. Often, a category of 'other' will appear to make up the whole.

Example

Display the information from the frequency distribution table above as a circle graph.

Solution
1. To find each sector, divide the frequency by the total and multiply by 36.

Choice of facility	Frequency	Degrees out of 360°
Recording studio	3	$\frac{3}{36} \times 360° = 30°$
Media lounge	7	$\frac{7}{36} \times 360° = 70°$
Sports equipment	9	$\frac{9}{36} \times 360° = 90°$
Shaded outdoor facilities with comfortable furniture	12	$\frac{12}{36} \times 360° = 120°$
Hire a well-known band for a school party	5	$\frac{5}{36} \times 360° = 50°$
Total	36	360°

2. Draw this graph by using either a *protractor* or a *computer*. Using the computer gives a graph that is both more accurate and better presented.

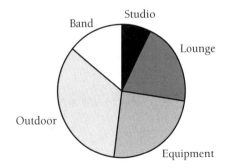

Student facilities

STATISTICAL MEASURES

Mean and median
The statistics that we most often read about and use in society are a summarised form of data. The first measures, the **mean** and the **median**, are called measures of **central tendency**.
- The mean is the sum of all the scores divided by the number of scores. It is often called the average.

$$\text{Mean} = \frac{\text{Sum of scores}}{\text{Number of scores}}$$

- The median is the middle score when the scores are placed in order.

$$\text{Median} = \text{Middle score}$$

Mode
The **mode** is the score that occurs most often in a distribution. It is the score with the *highest frequency*. If a group of numbers has two scores with the highest frequency the distribution is said to be **bimodal**.

Range
The range is a measure of the *spread* of the distribution.

$$\text{Range} = \text{Largest score} - \text{Smallest score}$$

Statistical measures of a small group of scores

Example
For the following scores find the mean, median, mode and range: 85, 74, 95, 88, 82, 88.

Solution
Manual calculation
- Mean = $\dfrac{85 + 74 + 95 + 88 + 82 + 88}{6}$ = 85.33
- Median: Put the scores in order from smallest to largest: 74, 82, 85, 88, 88, 95.
  Mark off scores from either end until middle score is reached: 74̸, 8̸2̸, 85, 88, 8̸8̸, 9̸5̸.
  There are two middle scores, 85 and 88.
  Take the average. Median = $\dfrac{85 + 88}{2}$ = 86.5
- Mode = 88. It occurs twice.
- Range = largest score − smallest score
  = 95 − 74
  = 21

Using the Casio 9850 graphics calculator
1. Press $\boxed{\text{MENU}}$ $\boxed{\text{STAT}}$ and enter the information from the list into List 1 using arrow keys and $\boxed{\text{EXE}}$ after each entry.
2. Press $\boxed{\text{F2}}$ CALC.
3. Press $\boxed{\text{F6}}$ SET.
4. Press 1 VAR XLIST: List 1 (as the data is in List 1).

5. Press 1 VAR Freq: 1 (ignore the other entries).
6. Press EXIT until the menu at the bottom shows GRPH CALC TEST INTR DIST.
7. Press F2 CALC.
8. Press F1 1 VAR (since there is only one list of numbers).

Statistical measures will appear on the screen.
- The *mean* is represented by $\bar{x}$ = 85.333333.
- The *median* is represented by Med = 86.5   *You may need to use the arrow keys to scroll down to find this entry.*
- The *mode* is represented by Mod = 88.   *Note that the calculator can only cope if there is a mode and only one mode. Otherwise it gives an incorrect answer.*
- The *range* is found by X max – X min = 95 – 74 = 21.

Example

Find the median of these test scores: 85, 74, 95, 96, 88, 82, 88.

Solution
Again put the scores in order from smallest to largest: 74, 82, 85, 88, 88, 95, 96.
Mark off scores from either end until middle score is reached: 74, 82, 85, 88, 88, 95, 96.
This time there is only one middle score: 88 is the median.

Example

Find the mode of the following scores: 85, 85, 74, 95, 96, 88, 82, 88.

Solution
There are two most common scores for this distribution. They are 88 and 85. The distribution is bimodal.

Statistical measures of a larger number of scores

$$\text{Mean of a large distribution} = \frac{\sum fx}{\sum f}$$

Example

Find the mean, median, mode and range of the following distribution: 4, 6, 5, 7, 7, 8, 5, 7, 8, 7, 8, 7.

Solution
Manual calculation
- Mean

Score (x)	Frequency (f)	f × x
4	1	4
5	2	10
6	1	6
7	5	35
8	3	24
	$\sum f = 12$	$\sum fx = 79$

$$\text{Mean} = \frac{\sum fx}{\sum f} = \frac{79}{12} = 6.58$$

- **Median**: Add a *cumulative frequency* column, which adds the number of scores as the table progresses.

Score (x)	Frequency (f)	cf
4	1	1 (score 1)
5	2	3 (scores 2 & 3)
6	1	4 (score 4)
7	5	9 (scores 5, 6, 7, 8 and 9)
8	3	12
	$\sum f = 12$	$\dfrac{n+1}{2} = \dfrac{\sum f + 1}{2} = 6.5$

The 6.5th score is in this section.

Hence, the median score = 7.

- **Mode** is the score with the highest frequency, which is also 7. This score has a frequency of 5.
- **Range** Largest score − smallest score = 8 − 4 = 4

Using the Casio 9850 graphics calculator

1. Press MENU STAT (enter information into lists, scores in list 1 and frequencies in list 2 using arrow keys and EXE).
2. Press F2 CALC F6 SET.
3. Press 1 VAR Xlist: LIST 1 (or whatever list has the data).
4. Press 1 VAR Freq: List 2 (or whatever list has the frequencies).
5. Press EXIT .
6. Press F2 CALC.
7. Press F1 1 VAR.

The Screen gives the mean, median (Med) and mode, and the range can be found by X max − X min. Scroll down using the arrow key to see all.

Quartiles

Upper and lower quartiles

The upper (or 3rd) quartile lies one-quarter of the way from the top of the distribution and the lower (or 1st) quartile lies one-quarter of the way from the bottom of the distribution. For the distribution 74, 82, 85, 88, 88, 95, the lower quartile is 82 and the upper quartile is 88.

The interquartile range represents 50% of the data.

$$\text{Interquartile range} = \text{Upper quartile} - \text{Lowest quartile}$$

For the data above interquartile range = 88 − 82 = 6

This value can give a better indication of the spread of scores when there are extreme scores that make the range seem much bigger than it might be without them.

Box and whisker plot

A **box and whisker plot** is a simple diagram that gives an idea of the spread of data. It shows the lowest score, the highest score, the median, the 1st quartile and the 3rd quartile. A box and whisker plot is sometimes called the *five number summary*.

Example

Draw a box and whisker plot for these scores: 63, 70, 75, 75, 76, 78, 78, 82, 82, 84, 85, 86, 87, 87, 88, 89, 92, 96, 104, 119

Solution

[63, 70, 75, 75, 76, 78, 78, 82, 82, 84] [85, 86, 87, 87, 88, 89, 92, 96, 104, 119]

Lowest score = 63   Median = 84.5   Highest score = 119

The lower quartile is halfway between 76 and 78, and is thus 77. The upper quartile is halfway between 88 and 89 and is thus 88.5. Mark these values on a number line and draw the box as shown.

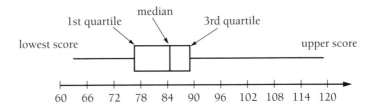

Using the Casio graphics calculator

1. Press MENU STAT EXE (enter the data into list 1 by pressing EXE after each score).
2. Press F1 GRAPH F6 SET.
3. Make sure it says StatGraph1 at the top of the screen.
4. Use the arrow keys to move the cursor down to G-Type and press F2 for Box. You may again need to press the arrow at F6 to find Box (called MedBox) at the bottom of the screen.
5. Press Xlist: List 1 F1.
6. Press Freq:1.
7. Press EXIT.
8. Press GPH1 F1.

   The box appears on the screen. To find the five values in the box and whisker plot:

   Press SHIFT F1. Trace to find the points as follows: lowest score = 63; lower quartile = 77; median = 84.5; upper quartile = 88.5; highest score = 119.

Features of box and whisker plots

- The length of the box surrounds the first and third quartiles. Hence, it is a good indication of the *degree of spread* (interquartile range). This may relate to *consistency* of performance. Data from the first box and whisker plot here has a far greater spread than that from the second.

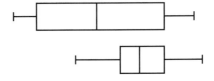

- The position of the box is an indication of *overall performance*. If a box is right of another, it generally indicates a better performance. In these boxes, the first set of data outperforms the second.

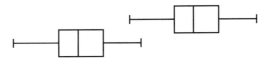

- The distance between the extremes of the whiskers indicates the *range* within a set of data. The extremes of the whiskers are at the *lower* and *upper* scores. This may give evidence of the *level of improvement* if the results are different efforts of the same product. In this plot, a considerable range is evident.

- Observations may be made about the percentage of scores in a particular category by using the line markers for the lower quartile, upper quartile and median. In this case, 75% of the scores of the second distribution are placed below the median of the first distribution.

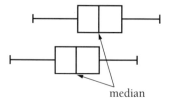

median

18 Probability

THE LANGUAGE OF PROBABILITY

Probability statements are statements about the likelihood, the **chance** or the **probability** of something happening. Some of the terms used when describing the probability of an event are: very likely; certain, equal chance, unlikely, no possibility, some chance.

All probability values lie between 0 and 1. 0 is used for an event that can never happen, and 1 is used for an event that will always happen. For example, throwing a 7 on a die with six sides would have a probability of 0. Getting either a head or a tail on the toss of a coin would have a probability of 1.

Example

Write the following probabilities in (i) words and (ii) values.
(a) What is the probability that you will get 'heads' when a coin is tossed?
(b) What is the probability that you will be a movie star by this time next year?

Solution
(a) (i) There is an equal chance that this will happen.
　　(ii) $\frac{1}{2}$ or 0.5
(b) (i) Unlikely
　　(ii) Probably less than $\frac{1}{1\,000\,000}$ or 0.000 001

EXPERIMENTAL PROBABILITY

Experimental probability occurs when the results are found by doing the experiment. Each occurrence of the experiment is called a **trial**. To find the probability of getting a 1 on the throw of a six-sided die, we conduct the experiment a number of times to see what the result is. In experimental probability, we count the number of times or *frequency* that 1 occurs.

Getting a 1 is called an **outcome**, that is, one of the possible results of the trial. The other outcomes would be: getting a 2, getting a 3, getting a 4, getting a 5 and getting a 6. The set of all possible outcomes is called the **sample space**. The more times an experiment is repeated, the greater the reliability of the data collected.

$$\text{Relative frequency of an outcome} = \frac{\text{Number of times outcome occurs}}{\text{Number of trials}} \times 100\%$$

For easy analysis, results are put into a **relative frequency table**.

Example

A six-sided die was thrown 200 times. The data obtained are shown in this relative table.

Outcome	1	2	3	4	5	6
Frequency	40	33	35	30	27	35
Relative frequency	$\frac{40}{200} \times 100\%$ = 20%	$\frac{33}{200} \times 100\%$ = 16.5%	$\frac{35}{200} \times 100\%$ = 17.5%	$\frac{30}{200} \times 100\%$ = 15%	$\frac{27}{200} \times 100\%$ = 13.5%	$\frac{35}{200} \times 100\%$ = 17.5%

(a) What is the frequency of getting a 5?
(b) How many trials were there in the experiment?
(c) What is the sample space?
(d) What is the relative frequency of getting the outcome of 1?

Solution
(a) A 5 occurs 27 times.
(b) There were 200 trials in the experiment.
(c) The sample space is {1, 2, 3, 4, 5, 6}.
(d) The relative frequency of getting a 1 = 20%.

PROBABILITY OF AN EVENT

$$\text{Probability of an event } P(E) = \frac{\text{Number of favourable outcomes}}{\text{Total number of outcomes}}$$

Dice

A standard die has six faces, numbered 1 to 6. Each face is equally likely to occur. Therefore, the probability of getting a face of 1, for example, is $\frac{1}{6}$. This is written as:

$P(1) = \frac{1}{6}$. Similarly, $P(2) = \frac{1}{6}$, $P(3) = \frac{1}{6}$, $P(4) = \frac{1}{6}$, $P(5) = \frac{1}{6}$ and $P(6) = \frac{1}{6}$.

$$P(1) + P(2) + P(3) + P(4) + P(5) + P(6) = \frac{1}{6} + \frac{1}{6} + \frac{1}{6} + \frac{1}{6} + \frac{1}{6} + \frac{1}{6} = \frac{6}{6} = 1$$

Other dice are the:
- tetrahedron die, which has four faces, numbered 1 to 4
- octahedron die, which has eight faces, numbered 1 to 8

Unless told, you can assume that the die used is a standard six-sided die.

Pack of cards

Many probability questions deal with packs of cards. A pack of cards has the following:
- 52 cards
- 26 red cards and 26 black cards
- 13 cards each of hearts ♥ diamonds ♦ spades ♠ and clubs ♣
- 4 cards each of ace, 2, 3, 4, 5, 6, 7, 8, 9, 10, jack, queen, king

The drawing of each card is equally likely to occur. The probability of drawing a king of hearts is P(king of hearts) = $\frac{1}{52}$, and of drawing a 2 of diamonds is P(2 of diamonds) = $\frac{1}{52}$.

Coins

A coin has two possible outcomes—a head or a tail. Again, each outcome is equally likely to occur.

The probability of tossing a head is $P(H) = P(T) = \frac{1}{2} = 0.5$.

Spinners

A spinner is a regular polygon or circle with a pivot at its centre. Each outcome on the spinner is equally likely to occur.

The following spinner has six outcomes. Hence, $P(1) = \frac{1}{6}$, $P(2) = \frac{1}{6}$ and so on.

A more sophisticated spinner is the roulette wheel shown here.

Experimental probability of an event

The probabilities given above will only actually occur if an experimental situation or action is repeated a large number of times. For example, if a coin is tossed 10 times, we do not necessarily get five heads and five tails. However, the more times the experiment is repeated, the greater the likelihood that the expected probability of 0.5 will result.

For some probabilities the **rule of indifference** does not apply because the likelihood of any particular outcome is not the same. This is demonstrated by this bag of marbles, where the probability of getting a red marble is not the same as the probability of getting a blue or a white marble.

$P(\text{red}) = \frac{5}{12}$; $P(\text{white}) = \frac{4}{12} = \frac{1}{3}$; $P(\text{blue}) = \frac{3}{12} = \frac{1}{4}$

COMPOUND PROBABILITIES

Many probability questions involve finding the chance that a combination of events occur. The **multiplication theorem of probability** states that if A and B are two independent events:

$$P(A \text{ and } B) = P(A) \times P(B)$$

Independent events are those in which the outcome of one event does not affect the outcome of the other event. For example, the event that a baby is born a girl and that the next baby is born a boy are independent events. One event does not affect the other. Multiplication theorem questions use the words 'and', 'then' or 'followed by'.

Example

From a pack of cards, two cards are drawn. Cards are replaced after each draw. Find the probability of drawing a king and a queen.

Solution

These two events are independent since the cards are replaced after the draw.

$P(\text{king}) = \frac{4}{52}$ $P(\text{queen}) = \frac{4}{52}$

Hence, $P(\text{king and queen}) = \frac{4}{52} \times \frac{4}{52}$

$= \frac{16}{2704}$

$= \frac{1}{169}$

Example

From a pack of cards, two cards are drawn. Cards are not replaced after each draw. Find the probability of drawing a king and a queen.

Solution

Although these two events are not independent, since the cards are not replaced after the draw, we can solve the problem in a similar way.

$P(\text{king and queen}) = \frac{4}{52} \times \frac{4}{51}$ *If the card is not replaced, there are only 51 cards from which to draw the second time.*

$= \frac{16}{2652}$

$= \frac{4}{663}$

The **addition theorem** of probability states that:

$$P(A \text{ or } B) = P(A) + P(B) - P(A \text{ and } B)$$

Addition theorem questions most often use the word 'or'.

Example

From a pack of cards, find the probability of drawing a king or a queen.

Solution

There are four kings in a pack of cards, so $P(\text{king}) = \frac{4}{52}$

There are four queens in a pack of cards, so $P(\text{queen}) = \frac{4}{52}$

$P(\text{king or queen}) = P(\text{king}) + P(\text{queen}) - P(\text{both king and queen at the same time})$

$= \frac{4}{52} + \frac{4}{52} - \frac{0}{52}$ *It is not possible to get both a king and a queen on the same card.*

$= \frac{8}{52}$

$= \frac{2}{13}$

Example

From a pack of cards find the probability of drawing a king or a heart.

Solution

There are four kings in a pack of cards, so $P(\text{king}) = \frac{4}{52}$

There are 13 hearts cards in a pack of cards, so $P(\text{heart}) = \frac{13}{52}$

$P(\text{king or heart}) = P(\text{king}) + P(\text{heart}) - P(\text{both king and heart})$

$= \frac{4}{52} + \frac{13}{52} - \frac{1}{52}$ *There is only one card that is both a king and a heart.*

$= \frac{4}{13}$

COMPLEMENTARY EVENTS

If E is an event, then 'not E' is its complementary event. The following are examples of complementary events.

Event	Complement
Throwing the number 4 on a standard die.	Not throwing the number 4 on a standard die, *or* throwing the numbers 1, 2, 3, 5 or 6 on a standard die.
Getting a head on the toss of a coin.	Not getting a head on the toss of a coin, *or* getting a tail on the toss of a coin.

Example

For each of the following events, state its complement and find the probability of both the event and its complement.
(a)   Drawing a heart from a pack of cards.
(b)   Getting a number less than 3 on the throw of a standard die.

Solution

Event	Probability	Complement	Probability
(a) Drawing a heart from a pack of cards.	$\frac{13}{52} = \frac{1}{4}$	Not drawing a heart from a pack of cards, *or* drawing a diamond, club or spade from a pack of cards.	$\frac{39}{52} = \frac{3}{4}$
(b) Getting a number less than 3 on the throw of a standard die.	$\frac{2}{6} = \frac{1}{3}$	Not getting a number less than 3 on the throw of a standard die, *or* getting a number 3 or bigger.	$\frac{4}{6} = \frac{2}{3}$

For the above examples it can be seen that the sum of the event and its complement is always 1, as in $\frac{1}{4} + \frac{3}{4} = \frac{4}{4} = 1$ and $\frac{1}{3} + \frac{2}{3} = \frac{3}{3} = 1$. This is always the case.

$$P(\text{not } E) = 1 - P(E) \text{ for all events } E$$

The complement of E may be written as: $P(\overline{E})$.

Example

Find the probability of not drawing a king from a pack of cards.

Solution

$P(\text{not drawing a king}) = 1 - P(\text{getting a king})$

$= 1 - \frac{4}{52}$

$= \frac{12}{13}$

Odds

If the probability of an event happening is $\frac{1}{4}$ then the probability of its complement is $\frac{3}{4}$. This is written as the **odds** are 1 : 3.

Example

If the odds are 5 : 3
(a) how many outcomes are there in the sample space?
(b) what is probability of success and the probability of failure?

Solution
(a) There are 5 + 3 = 8 outcomes in the sample space.
(b) $P(\text{success}) = \frac{5}{5+3} = \frac{5}{8}$ and hence $P(\text{failure}) = \frac{3}{8}$

Grids and tree diagrams

Grids and tree diagrams can be used to help when answering probability questions. A **grid** is used when only *two* choices are to be made. A **tree diagram** is used when more than *two* choices are to be made.

Example

(a) List the possible outcomes when two dice are thrown, and state the number in the sample space.
(b) Find the probability that both numbers are even.

Solution
(a)

	1	2	3	4	5	6
1	1, 1	1, 2	1, 3	1, 4	1, 5	1, 6
2	2, 1	2, 2	2, 3	2, 4	2, 5	2, 6
3	3, 1	3, 2	3, 3	3, 4	3, 5	3, 6
4	4, 1	4, 2	4, 3	4, 4	4, 5	4, 6
5	5, 1	5, 2	5, 3	5, 4	5, 5	5, 6
6	6, 1	6, 2	6, 3	6, 4	6, 5	6, 6

1 on the first die and 6 on the second die.

(b) P(both numbers are even) = $\frac{9}{36} = \frac{1}{4}$

There are 36 in the sample space of all possibilities.

Example

To do his assignment, Eli has a choice of a desktop or laptop computer, a laser or dot matrix printer and white or blue paper.
(a) How many different combinations of choices does he have?
(b) What is the chance that he uses a laptop computer and blue paper?

Solution
(a)

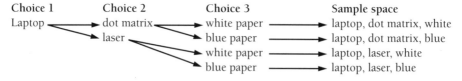

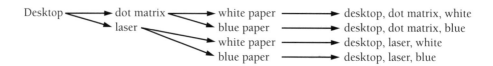

There are 8 choices in the sample space.

(b) P(laptop and blue) = $\frac{2}{8} = \frac{1}{4}$ *As seen by the arrows in the sample space.*

TI calculator conversions

TEXAS INSTRUMENTS KEYSTROKES FOR SCIENTIFIC AND GRAPHICS CALCULATORS

Page 5. Adding and subtracting integers

Integer Problem	Diagram	Answer	Notes and calculator steps (for Texas TI – 30X IIB)
6 – –2 = 6 + 2	△△△△△△ △△	8	6 – (–2) =

Page 8. Calculator use and time

It is usually marked as $\boxed{° \, ' \, ''}$ on Texas (the same as Casio).

Page 15–18. Converting from an improper fraction to a mixed number

Calculator Steps: 7 $\boxed{A^b/_c}$ 4 = and likewise for other calculations involving fractions on these pages.

Page 25. Linking per cent, decimals and fractions

(ii) Calculator steps: 65 $\boxed{A^b/_c}$ 100 = To get the fraction form of the answer you must use the $\boxed{A^b/_c}$ button.

Page 63. Scientific notation (standard form) on the calculator

To enter numbers in scientific notation on the calculator use the $\boxed{\text{2nd}}$ $\boxed{\text{SCI/ENG}}$ buttons and select $\boxed{\text{SCI}}$.

To enter 3 456 897 031 simply press $\boxed{\text{2nd}}$ $\boxed{\text{SCI/ENG}}$ $\boxed{\text{SCI}}$ and enter the number. The calculator will then convert it to scientific notation.

Page 79. Methods of sketching a straight line (TI 83 and 83 Plus)

(a) Use $\boxed{\text{2nd}}$ $\boxed{\text{MEM}}$ → $\boxed{\text{RESET}}$ → $\boxed{\text{ALL RAM}}$ → $\boxed{\text{RESET}}$ to clear the calculator.
(b) Press $\boxed{Y=}$ and enter $Y_1 = 3$ $\boxed{X, T, θ, n}$ – 5
(c) Press $\boxed{\text{WINDOW}}$ and set the Domain (X values) and Range (Y values) as required.
(d) Press $\boxed{\text{GRAPH}}$.
(e) Press $\boxed{\text{TRACE}}$ and $\boxed{◀}$ or $\boxed{▶}$ to trace along the graph.
(f) The $\boxed{\text{ZOOM}}$ button, $\boxed{\text{ZOOM-IN}}$ and $\boxed{▲}$, $\boxed{▼}$, $\boxed{◀}$ and $\boxed{▶}$ can be used to find accurate intercepts.

Pages 84–86. Solving simultaneous equations

(a) Follow the procedure for graphing a straight line (p. 79) and enter $Y_1 = $ $\boxed{X, T, θ, n}$ and $Y_2 = 2$ $\boxed{X, T, θ, n}$ – 1
(b) Adjust the $\boxed{\text{WINDOW}}$ settings.
(c) To find the intersection of the two lines $\boxed{\text{TRACE}}$ and $\boxed{◀}$ or $\boxed{▶}$.
(d) To check the intersection press the $\boxed{\text{ZOOM}}$ button, $\boxed{\text{ZOOM-IN}}$ and $\boxed{▲}$, $\boxed{▼}$, $\boxed{◀}$ or $\boxed{▶}$.

Mathematics Dictionary   TI calculator conversions

Page 88. Solving quadratic equations

(a) Press [MATH] [0] to get into the Equation Solver function. The screen will then read eqn : 0 =
(b) Enter 2 [X, T, θ] [X²] + 9 [X, T, θ, n] − 5. Instead of using the [X²] function you can use [^] [2].
(c) Press [ENTER] to get the boundaries and [X =] will appear.
(d) The Equation Solver expects you to guess the solutions. You may enter [X = 1].
(e) Press [ALPHA] [ENTER] and the response [X = 0.5] will appear.
(f) Enter another guess, e.g. [X = 6] and the other solution [X = 5] will appear.

Page 89. Graphing (sketching) parabolas

(a) Select [Y =] and enter $Y_1 = 2 - 3$ [X, T, θ, n] + [X, T, θ, n] [X²].
(b) Check the [WINDOW] settings and press [GRAPH].
(c) Use the [TRACE] function and ◄ or ► to trace along the graph to find the intercepts.
(d) To check the intercepts press the [ZOOM] button, [ZOOM-IN] and ▲, ▼, ◄ or ►.

Page 112. The tangent ratio—finding tan ratios with the calculator

Calculator steps: [TAN] [14°] = 0.25

Pages 113 & 114. Finding unknown angles and sides

Use the [2nd F] [TAN] [A^b/$_c$] buttons on your calculator.

Page 114. Sine (sin) and cosine (cos) ratios

Use the [SIN] button on your calculator to get 0.5

Page 115. Use the [2nd F] [SIN] [A^b/$_c$] buttons on your calculator

On the calculator press [COS] 30 =

Page 120. Bar or column graphs

1. Press [STAT] [EDIT] and enter the information into [L1] using the [ENTER] button or ▼. Press [2nd] [Y =] [STAT PLOT] [1] [ENTER] [(Plot 1)] [ON] [ENTER] to turn the first stat plot on.
2. Select the appropriate type (vertical bar graph) from the options (scatter plot, line graph, histogram, box plot with outliers, box plot with whiskers and data list) and [ENTER].
3. Check the [WINDOW] settings to fit the data in [L1] and press [GRAPH].
4. Use the [TRACE], [ZOOM] and [ZOOM-IN] functions plus ▲, ▼, ◄ or ► to locate values on the graph.

Page 124. Statistical measures of a small group of scores

1. Press [STAT] [EDIT] and enter data in [L1].
2. Press [STAT] [CALC] and select [1-VAR STATS (L1)]. Press [ENTER].
3. The screen shows the mean (x), the sum of the scores ($\sum x$), the sample standard deviation (Sx), the population standard deviation (σx), the number of scores entered (n), the minimum (min x), the first quartile (Q1), the median (Med), the third quartile (Q3) and the maximum (max x).

Page 125. Statistical measures of a larger number of scores

1. Press [STAT] [EDIT] and enter data in [L1] with the frequencies in [L2].
2. Press [STAT] [CALC] and select [1-VAR STATS (L1 L2)]. Press [ENTER].

Page 126. Box and whisker plots

1. Press [STAT] [EDIT] and enter data in [L1].
2. Press [2nd] [Y=] and select a plot by choosing [ON]. You can operate three plots at once if needed.
3. Choose the box and whisker plot.
4. Check the [WINDOW] settings to fit the data in [L1] and press [GRAPH].
5. Use the [TRACE] [ZOOM] and [ZOOM-IN] functions plus ◄ or ► to locate the five number summary (minimum, Quartile 1, median, Quartile 3 and maximum) on the graph.